I0211164

Uncommon Vessels

Uncommon Vessels

The Ongoing Journey to a Renewed Mind

SARA WHITTEN

RESOURCE *Publications* · Eugene, Oregon

UNCOMMON VESSELS
The Ongoing Journey to a Renewed Mind

Copyright © 2022 Sara Whitten. All rights reserved. Except for brief quotations in critical publications or reviews, no part of this book may be reproduced in any manner without prior written permission from the publisher. Write: Permissions, Wipf and Stock Publishers, 199 W. 8th Ave., Suite 3, Eugene, OR 97401.

Resource Publications
An Imprint of Wipf and Stock Publishers
199 W. 8th Ave., Suite 3
Eugene, OR 97401

www.wipfandstock.com

PAPERBACK ISBN: 978-1-6667-3512-3
HARDCOVER ISBN: 978-1-6667-9188-4
EBOOK ISBN: 978-1-6667-9189-1

FEBRUARY 8, 2022 3:15 PM

Scriptures taken from the Holy Bible, New International Version®, NIV®. Copyright © 1973, 1978, 1984, 2011 by Biblica, Inc.™ Used by permission of Zondervan. All rights reserved worldwide. www.zondervan.com The "NIV" and "New International Version" are trademarks registered in the United States Patent and Trademark Office by Biblica, Inc.™

Languages references from:

Strong, James. "Offering." *Strong's Expanded Exhaustive Concordance of the Bible*. Nashville: Thomas Nelson, 2009. Print.

CONTENTS

Prologue

Dear friend,

If you are holding this book, it is for a reason. My ongoing prayer is that you will not finish this book in the same way that you started it.

I pray the Lord will renew your mind and your hope in order that you may be a *truly* uncommon vessel.

Love and blessings,

ACKNOWLEDGEMENTS

Deepest gratitude to my husband, Garrett, for watching our babies and drying many tears in order that this dream could become a reality.

Thank you also to Theresa, Caroline, Robert, and Harry for the encouragement, help, and prophetic stewardship that ultimately led to the completion of this book.

To God be *all* the glory, the honor, and the power forever.

INTRODUCTION

WHAT'S IN A NAME?

"UNCOMMON," I SAID DECISIVELY from the passenger seat as my husband turned into the mall parking lot. "If God used me to write a book, I think He would call it *Uncommon*." I loved the way that word *felt*. Like the beginning of a Marvel movie when the character first discovers he or she has a super power, the word "uncommon" carries with it the butterflies-in-your-stomach and goosebumps-on-your-arms feeling of a life destined for adventure and greater purpose. Also, it sounded much better than the alternative option of "Becoming Weird," though some days that title seems more accurate.

After much deliberation, I decided my journey with God could be summed up in having my mind blown by God's realness, and henceforth being wrecked forever desiring normalcy again. The *ongoing* process of a mind being transformed. I say "ongoing" because I certainly make no claims of having arrived. In fact, this book sat mostly written on my laptop for years for fear of releasing it without it including all I wanted to include. There was just never an end to the new things God was doing and showing me! God has reminded me, however, that the closest I can get to "completion" is a snapshot on my journey that may somehow—in God's crazy way of doing things—align with the snapshot in your journey in a way that refreshes and encourages and sharpens.

This is a book of testimony, really. Sweet truths of the Bible illuminated in parables God has enacted through my life. The process of learning how to live in an *uncommon* way, the word that ended up naming this book. So don't read this book as polished preaching from someone who has always "gotten it right," written in a clean, quiet office. Read this book for what it is. Words typed one-handed as I balance our second baby on my lap with crumbs on our floor, sins in my past, and scars on my heart. A book that flows not from expertise but from the uncontainable gratitude of someone saved by grace who God decided He could still use.

The answer to the famed Shakespearian question, "What's in a name?" is quite a bit, actually. Biblically, when Adam named the animals (Genesis 2:19), it was more profound than just associating sounds with a creature. The implication of the original texts is that by naming the animal, Adam was capturing its nature, its purpose, its function. Throughout the Bible, names are also reminders. When Sarah's son was named Isaac, it was to remind her that what she had laughed off as impossible was brought about by God. Jacob's name was changed to Israel to signify a complete transformation of character, as was Saul to Paul. The list is literally long enough to be its own book, but God was making a point. Just as the name of a person or animal captures its purpose, the title of this book needed to capture its purpose.

This book's purpose is to impart thoughts that I cannot take credit for. In fact, God's teaching in my life has been quite contrary to my own, and it has taken more than a few "laps around the mountain" to accept it. God did a Romans 12:2 turnaround in my life, and as He drops these little nuggets of truth into my life, I turn with cupped hands and extend it to you in hopes that it may transform you as well. To call out the identity and purpose already dormant in *you*, to create Kingdom thinkers, and as a result, create some truly uncommon people. A group of sacred vessels to have God's power, love, and wisdom poured into them who could then take it to a hungry world. *Uncommon Vessels*. Thus began a haphazard leap of faith to share what I can only describe as the messy journey of discovering the meaning of the renewed mind Romans

12:2 references. The verse we all hear but rarely ever *hear*. As you begin this quest, open your heart, open your mind, and prepare to be forever changed.

Chapter One

THE BOW AND ARROW

Do not conform to the pattern of this world, but be transformed by the renewing of your mind. Then you will be able to test and approve what God's will is—His good, pleasing, and perfect will.

ROMANS 12:2

QUALITY CONTROL

WHY DOES OUR MIND need renewal anyway? What strikes me about the common verse from Romans 12:2 is that second sentence. It's the "why." Like most toddlers, I spent most of my time asking "why" and truly wanting to understand. In this case, the "why" is promptly and plainly stated. God wants us to be able to *test* and *approve* His will. Wow! Merriam Webster defines "test" as "a procedure . . . used to identify or characterize a substance or constituent" and "the procedure of submitting a statement to such conditions or operations as will lead to its proof or disproof or to its acceptance or rejection." When we look at "approve" in Webster's, it is to "give formal or official sanction." Going a level deeper, Webster' definition of "sanction" is pretty intense. It's decreeing, agreeing, or making a binding oath. Sanctions in the natural often

1

dictate military and economic operations. Having a renewed mind effectively means discerning and enforcing where God wants our efforts and our resources. A renewed mind is the tool that allows us to decree, agree, and bind ourselves to God's will by being able to know what God's will is and what isn't God's will. A renewed mind, in essence, allows us to be Heaven's quality control.

We can take a thought, word, action, or event, and have a basis by which to accept or reject it as "yes, this fits God's will" or "no, this doesn't fit God's will." Understanding God's will in a situation (to the best of our ability . . . let's be honest, we all get "off" sometimes . . .) is absolutely vital. It tells us when to fight, when to be still, when to agree, when to reject, when to hold, and when to release. The cool part about each definition I just explored is it inevitably leads to *action*. A renewed mind and what we think with it inevitably determines what we do. And what we do sets the course for not only our lives but the eternal story the Lord is writing.

STRAIGHT TO THE SOURCE

Walking with the trinity is like walking on the stars. I say this because for either one you must turn your whole world upside down. There is no prescription or one-size-fits-all life plan. I believe He made us uniquely so that we would *have* to go straight to the source.

Picking up a new book makes my heart race. On bated breath, I read through the first chapter. Sometimes the overwhelming excitement of the new journey has my book sitting abandoned on the dashboard, forever waiting to the "perfect moment" of undivided attention it deserves. The truth is, however, that I could possess entire libraries. I could have read every testimony, every technique, every morsel of wisdom from those who have walked with the Lord before me, yet if I did not directly seek the Lord, I would only know *about* Him. I wouldn't know Him. As life-giving as it is to read about testimonies or wisdom from the lives of others, there are specific purposes and plans for *your* life that you will never read about or hear about unless you dive in with the Author of them.

KNOWING GOD

The request I get more than any other from those who submit prayers requests online is simply, "I want to know God's will for my life." Knowing God's will starts with knowing God. Imagine you spend your life researching George Washington. You learn every detail that can be discovered. You pour over documentaries and research papers. You even travel to be in the same places he did when he lived. Now imagine getting to meet him. There is something intangible about that direct contact. The rumors are clarified. The stories are brought to life. The wrinkle of his nose when he laughs and the inflection with which he speaks bring his character to life. The questions you have can be asked directly instead of hunting in research archives hoping to piece together your own guess at an answer. You get an *emotional* impression. You can decide how you feel about him. You can decide if you see in him similarities to yourself or others you know. Direct connection revolutionizes your understanding of someone. Knowledge does not illicit love. Experience does. So, when looking for the answer to "what is God's will for me?" or "what is my purpose," we must first start with "how do I hear God?"

I don't know where you personally fall on the spectrum of familiarity with the prophetic. Some of you may be way further along than me. Others of you may be discovering for the first time that God talks back. To others of you, it may just be a new name for that thing you've always done, like noticing that still small voice or the unction in your gut. For clarity's sake, let's talk about what the prophetic is. Prophesy is a receiving a message from God. It may come directly to you. It may be delivered through another's mouth. It will never contradict God's Word or God's character. Its intention is to remind you of your identity, give you hope, redirect you, or confirm what you've been hearing. You have the gift of prophesy. How do I know? Biblically, Jesus's sacrifice made it so that we don't need a high priest. We are removed from the days of Moses and the tent of meeting. Instead, the Holy Spirit sets up a tent of meeting within us. We are restored to the direct communication enjoyed before the fall, and this direct communication revolutionizes our understanding of everything. It makes it possible to fall in love with God. But it's even more than that. Since it's God we're talking about and not just a historical character, we are talking about our very Creator. Direct contact means we can ask the most important questions of all. These are the questions that burn within us regardless of who we are. We all ache to know the answers of "who am I?" and "what is my purpose?"

BOW AND ARROW

There are three major essentials of a bow and arrow. All three were highlighted to me as I gripped my camp chair armrests with white knuckles and watched my seven-year-old son do target practice. To do anything long range you must have arrows, a bow, and someone putting strength behind them. Arrows are like the things we do in this life. They are our purposes with a lower-case "p." You leading that vacation Bible school team is a purpose God has for you. It's not the *only* purpose on your life, though. Often, I hear people asking what their purpose is, but they are really seeking a different answer. Our purposes are many and often are seasonal. Our identity, however, is unchanging.

The bow from which we launch these arrows is our identity. It's what puts directionality into what we do. It is not interchangeable with the seasons, though we may understand it in a deeper fullness from one season to the next. It also gives our efforts longevity. Picture throwing an arrow by hand. Now contrast that with launching an arrow. In battle, arrows become a game changer because they made it possible to attack from long range as opposed to being limited to hand-to-hand combat. When we act out of our God-created design, we don't fatigue in our purposes. Also, the force of our efforts is magnified when we walk in our identity. They become an expression of our natural gifts and desires.

Both bow and arrows would do nothing unless used. Can you go your whole life and do nothing with your identity and purpose? I suppose you could. Would that change the fact that you still *have* an identity and purpose? Absolutely not. The first question you should ask yourself is are you tapping into your God-created identity and purposes? The second question takes it one step farther and asks whose hands are you letting power your shot?

We can be a bow and arrows in the hands of the Lord, letting His strength power our efforts. While these times are not without resistance, we recognize His supernatural opening of opportunities and His accomplishment of what we could not do on our own. Speaking of doing things on our own, we also have the power to "do it ourselves," using our identity in line with our ideas and launching arrows aimlessly, hoping for success. This often leaves us tired and feeling stuck. Finally, we can also be highjacked by the enemy, letting him manipulate our gifts and efforts in an effort to keep us from our greatest expression of ourselves. If you've ever heard that the areas of your greatest attack are often linked to your areas of greatest calling, my life is living proof of this. What ways have attacks made you shy away from the very ways God wants to use you most? Have you been wounded and isolated yourself from people when you were made to be an influencer? There are many ways in which the enemy can whisper to us to change our aim, not use that arrow, or lay down our bow altogether.

In teaching our son archery, we had to teach him how to hold his arrows so he would not fumble them, how to balance his bow, and—most importantly—how to aim to hit the mark (while not injuring others along the way). Often, I think our own heavenly Father is doing the very same things in us. He is teaching us how to not fumble our missions, how to hold on to our identity effectively, and how to hit the mark while not injuring others along the way. Unlike me watching my son, however, I don't think God watches us with white knuckles, coaching from a camp chair. I think He is right there holding it with us, constantly speaking helpful direction, helping us recover from our mistakes, and cheering joyfully when we hit the mark.

THE PARADOX OF SAFETY

We all know the bows and arrows are not used for nap time. They're used for battle. I cannot talk about our identity and purposes as a bow and arrows without addressing the number one barrier to using them. The allure of safety. I've never heard it put better than from the mouths of Christians working in the 10/40 window. I've heard, "In the east the enemy appears as a roaring dragon, but in the west, he appears as an angel of light." In other words, in these countries where the gospel is scarce (which are often unsafe areas as well), there is a very real awareness of the spirit realm. Even those who don't know Jesus know that there are evil spirits. In contrast, in much of the western world, comfort and intellectualism lure people into apathy (angel of the light). No one wants to get their hands dirty for fear of what it might cost them, not realizing that by not doing so it is literally costing their life. It is all too easy to trade the adventures the Lord has for each one of us (whatever they may look like) for "normal," for "comfortable," and for "good." Another worker in a middle eastern nation put it this way: There is a satanic lullaby that plays very loudly in America. Satanic lullaby. Those words will forever stay with me. Lured by the sleepiness of comfort, not wanting anything more, and totally unaware of the incredible "more" that God has for us.

As medicine and modern convenience evolve more and more, there is a dangerous trend of "playing it safe." There are whole careers built on risk assessment. There is insurance for almost everything you can think of—even pets! The irony is that the Bible tells us the opposite. When were God's people the safest? When they were crossing through a sea suspended only by the Word of God, wandering in a forsaken desert, shipwrecked, bitten by snakes, ministering to the sick, in prison, or facing hostile authorities. In contrast, the Ananias and Sapphira's, the Jonah's, and the Judases tell us that seeking our own safety, insurance, or comfort actually sends us right into the heart of danger.

Now don't misunderstand this as a directive to seek danger and risk. Ultimately, you may be brave if you go cliff diving, but if the Lord didn't send you cliff diving, then you're missing the whole point. Risk and danger are not synonymous with "leaps of faith," but we must know that in accepting a life of faith we are guaranteed risks and stepping out of comfort zones (or being thrown out of comfort zones as sometimes happens) along the way.

For years I sought safety. Ironically, during these years I felt the least safe. I felt exposed to the elements of life and battered by wave after wave, regardless of how much I attempted to control my life. No matter how much I was tossed on the stormy seas of circumstance those years, I pretended to not hear Jesus calling me out on the water to Him and instead clung to the boat as if it was the safety on which my life depended. I was afraid of God's answers. I was afraid even more of if He didn't answer. I preferred to learn *about* Him from a safe distance rather than learning *from* Him. What I didn't know was that the safest place to be spiritually is not always the safest place to be circumstantially. The safest place is always in the center of God's will.

I have a ministry partner who should not be alive. She should write her own book, as her stories could not even fit in mine. She has been driven past the gallows by Al Qaeda yet ended up ministering to their leaders and walking away safely. She has lived in war zones spreading the gospel. She has escaped bullets and had to evacuate in the cover of night with a team that miraculously crossed a river without getting wet. Also, because she is so humble, she took years even telling me these testimonies. One thing she will always reiterate is that whenever God said "go," it was time to go. Regardless of the circumstances or the outcome. And He has never steered her wrong.

Many of us in our journeys catch ourselves in seasons of being too afraid to step out. Like the disciples who stayed in the boat and watched Peter walk on water. We want to see the miraculous from a safe distance that doesn't directly impact us if it goes south. Maybe it's from being burned the last time we took a leap of faith. Maybe it's from doubts about the One calling us out to walk on the proverbial waters and His trustworthiness or goodness. Maybe it's from a well-honed ability to simply tune out the voice that calls us out on the water. Maybe it's a loss of hunger and passion for what awaits us that makes taking the step of faith no longer seems worth it. For whatever reason, these seasons come. For you reading this, you may recall seasons like this. You may be *in* a season like this. You may have never yet in your life *left* the safe season. Now, my friend, is your time.

The saying "nothing ventured, nothing gained" certainly holds truth. If we never leave the safe season, we never taste the adventure or thrill of witnessing what we never knew was possible. Why then are there times that we venture out and fall flat? Why are there times that just *aren't* the happy Hollywood endings that somehow suddenly turn everything around? These experiences can leave us embittered, determined to never step out of the boat, comfortable in the safe place. By going through life ignoring direct engagement with God regarding the truth about our identity and purpose, we end up formulating our own hypotheses about how to flourish which only ever leave us empty.

ON PURPOSE

Years of studying Psychology and Counseling in my Bachelor's and Master's degrees can be boiled down to a basic underlying truth that runs through individual, marriage, and family emotional health; when purpose is lost, all else crumbles. When an individual loses purpose, connections falter, anxiety increases, and depression and hopelessness creep into the forefront. When a marriage loses purpose (loses common goals or loses sight of why they got together in the first place), criticism increases, joy turns into obligation, and after a while sometimes the two will even begin to wonder what they are doing together. When a family loses purpose, what was once a unit of shared identity and support ruptures and drift like ice caps on the water as each member floats off to do his or her own thing. Family members pass like ships in the night, sharing the same space but little of deep emotional consequence.

Like dominos in a line, the list goes on and on of what purpose affects. The greater purpose one feels in his or her career, the more likely he or she is to stick with it. The more purposeful two individuals are in a friendship (meaning being vocal about wanting to invest in the friendship, making a point to carve out time for each other), the more likely the friendship will weather the years. There are few phrases that soften hearts more than "this was meant to be" or "you are here for a reason." Why do we long to know that? We ache to have validity and even necessity in our work, in our relationships, in our presence, and in our very existence. We ache because we all have purposes that we long to regain. We are all on various points in the road of discovering these purposes because if you had already *completed* all God had in mind for you to do, then more than likely you would no longer be on this earth. Maybe you have unearthed whole mountains of your purposes thus far with the Lord. Maybe you've barely scratched the surface. Whatever the case may be, it is *essential* that you know that *you still have more to discover*. Wherever you are, say this aloud: "I have purposes. Right now. And they are vital." If you've gotten some inquisitive stares—congratulations—because you're starting to step out of the boat. I'm sure Peter got a few of those when he got ready to climb overboard. In the Introduction to this book, I told you I could've called this book "Becoming Weird." I was half joking. As we go down this road together, it is my sincere hope that you will finish unable to recall how you ever lived a "normal" life before.

WHO ARE YOU?

During my Master's, I was at an educational gathering of mostly people I did not know to learn more about a specific type of therapy. I smiled until my cheeks hurt and introduced myself. I filled a tiny paper plate with a few items from the vegetable and fruit tray and braced myself for a night of mildly uncomfortable small talk. Since it was a relatively small group, and the speaker was going to open up for discussion later, he asked us to each go around and introduce ourselves. There was a catch. We had to share who we were *without* saying what we did for a living or listing our hobbies. A few embarrassed laughs and glances around the room showed that we share a common discomfort in doing that. Such a simple question, but such a hard one to answer. Who are you? Your career and hobbies are what you do, not who you are. This is not identity. They can, however, give you clues to the answer to that ultimate question. Are you a mechanic? Maybe it's because who you are is someone who is a solver, someone who finds solutions, and someone whose thoughts are able to break down complex things in life to understand each little piece. Is gardening a hobby of yours? Maybe it's because you are a nurturer and have an innate ability to sense needs and meet them. While that's a start, our identities are way more complex than that. When you add in purpose, it's a complexity so profound our minds literally could not process it all.

> Such knowledge is too wonderful for me, too lofty for me
> to attain (Ps 139:6).

We, however, have a God whose thoughts are not even remotely like our processing abilities. So, since we cannot begin to process or unravel all the intricacies of our identities and purposes on our own, our sweet God reveals them to us layer by layer, piece by piece, in perfect timing, and as we are ready. He is the One who Psalm 139 says "knit us together in our mother's womb" (v. 13) has also "ordained" (v. 16) our days. Merriam-Webster defines ordain as "to establish or order by decree." That means just like we go to a restaurant and order a meal by describing and communicating what we want, God ordered our days. He speaks and creates and describes exactly what He wants for us. His greatest hopes and dreams for His children. Before we were made, He spoke our individual, unique, one-of-a-kind identity and all the purposes we could fulfill. Unlike our teenage phases , midlife crises, or ever-changing minds, since the moment He spoke these things over us, *they have not changed.*

> *The word of the Lord endures forever (Isa. 40:8).*

Our *perception* of who we were or what we were supposed to do may have changed many times, but God has held these jewels of our identity and purposes constantly in His hands...and He is ready to reveal them to you. The bow and arrow need the archer. We come alive in the hands of our Archer God. If you're aching to be used, it's not a matter of pushing ourselves to the point of mental fatigue "figuring it out." He knows how to use us perfectly. Just surrender, listen, and be ready to respond to what He says.

CONFLICT

My son's little fingers dove into the popcorn tub as he shoveled fistfuls into his toddler mouth. He had been fully engaged in the movie theater watching *The Good Dinosaur (2015)*, but now he felt the need to break the tension and power-eat his way through the emotions. His worried eyes fixated on the movie theater screen as the little dinosaur tumbled down stream, half-drowning, being carried away by rapid currents. Finally, his little heart couldn't take it anymore. "Is he gonna be ok, mommy?!?" he asks entirely too loudly in the theater. Laughter erupts around us. Our son has grown into ever the entertainer and family comedian, but truthfully his most comedic moments are when he says something so poignantly truthful that it's almost funny to hear out loud.

Everyone wants an epic life story. There is nothing wrong with that. The common rebuttal is "real life isn't like that." Oh really? I think most people forget that every fairy tale, every heroic movie, every epic adventure has a conflict. The conflict is that part of the movie that you start stress-eating your popcorn or the part of the book in which you shun interruptions in order to power through to a more palatable place to pause. It's the time where you worry that everything won't be ok. It's section in the plot at which you can't bear to stop. That's why cliffhangers or endings with un- resolved conflicts feel so dissatisfying.

Even the most well-done movies are still just movies. We can comfortably remove ourselves at the end, reminding ourselves it was only a story. Life is not so easy. We *are* the protagonist. Even though we are assured that everything will be ok (see Jeremiah 29:11 and Romans 8:28), we sometimes forget that assurance when we are physically walking through the conflict. And it is indeed a conflict. A war is being waged in the supernatural at all times, and we feel its reverberations. This war is primarily against you knowing your identity and purpose because the enemy knows that if we lose that, we lose effectiveness. In the heat of the trial, it's tempting to give up. We worry. Maybe it's too hard. Maybe it wasn't meant to be. Maybe it isn't a happy ending.

In the face of conflict what makes us persevere is knowing who wrote our story. You know what to expect theatrically from Michael Bay or George Lucas. We know, from the written accounts in the Bible of so many others' stories with the Lord, what to expect from God. The renewed mind looks at his or her own life like a God story. You are the main character. The villain of Heaven and earth is mad because you are affecting the world for good. The villain tries to stop you (hence why you feel the conflict). But the Savior steps in, defeats him, and *wins* for everyone. The renewed mind looks at the attacks of the enemy and sees that it can never be enough for defeat. The pathetic attempts to stop you are just affirmation that you're accomplishing your good works because you have gotten his attention. It makes it possible to understand how Paul could honestly call trials joy. It really becomes a joy once you see the victory they are trying to mask.

> Consider it pure joy, my brothers and sisters, whenever you face trials of many kinds, because you know that the testing of your faith produces perseverance. (James 1:2–3).

When you have perseverance, you do not give up, and when you do not give up, you get your happy ending. Because we are all part of one story, we all have parts to play, and in this story, we know the ending. Good wins. God wins. Life comes without relent. As Jesus warned in John 16:33, "In this world you will have trouble." He also said, which I think we have a harder time grasping, "take heart! I have overcome the world" (John 16:33).

> If anyone serves Me, he must follow Me; and where I am, My servant will be as well. If anyone serves Me, the Father will honor him. **Now My soul is troubled, and what shall I say?**

'Father save Me from this hour'? No, it is for this purpose
that I have come to this hour.

(John 12:26–28)

TAKE IT TO GOD:

At the close of each chapter there will be a chance to make it personal. Ask each of these questions one at a time, and wait in the
still silence for God's answer. Jot it down!

What part of your character do you want me to know in a
deeper way?

What is something I don't yet know about my identity or how
you see me?

What is a purpose you have for me right now?

In what ways are you calling me to step out of the boat beyond
my comfort zone?

Chapter Two

Our Superpower of Choice

"And you have your choices/ and these are what make man great/ His ladder to the stars"

-Mumford and Sons

"WALKING" IN FAITH

The entire gospel begins and ends with choices. Adam and Eve fell with a choice. We are redeemed with a choice to accept Jesus's sacrifice. There is a reason that being an uncommon vessel requires "taking up our cross" daily. It's because there is a picture painted in that that is *active*.

Just this morning (before I knew what I would be writing today), I was reading the passage in Genesis 13:15–17, in which the Lord tells Abraham to "walk the land." God says:

> *"All the land that you see I will give to you and your offspring forever. I will make your offspring like the dust of the earth, so that if anyone could count the dust, then your offspring could be counted. Go, walk through the length and breadth of the land, for I am giving it to you."*

I looked up the Hebrew for the word used for walk. I looked it up mostly because the word has such a high correlation with faith.

You hear things like "faith walk," or "walking in faith," or "walking by faith." I love Hebrew. Not only because its translation gets closer to what the original writers meant, but because it's a language of pictures. A picture is worth a thousand words, and the Hebrews knew that. Hold on because this is about to get deep. The stem of the word used here is transliterated as *"halak"*[1] which makes up half of the word used for "walk" here. This stem can be used to be a *reflexive action, reciprocal action,,* or *simple action.* Language nerds are freaking out right now, and everyone else is contemplating setting this book down. Stick with me. To walk his promised land, Abraham had to do something to himself (move his own legs), do something reciprocal (respond to God's directive to go and see), and do something simple (take a walk).

I think, personally, to walk in God's promises it takes a little bit of all three of these types of action that are tied together in this root word. Sometimes it'll be to do things to yourself (reflexive). Think spiritual growth, fine tuning ourselves, pruning those bad habits, stretching ourselves in our weak points.

Other times it will be choices to respond to an opportunity God has opened up (reciprocal). Even when Mary, mother of Jesus, was selected for that honor, it didn't just "happen" to her. She made the *choice* to *respond* to the opportunity the angel presented her with from the Lord. God makes a move. We have the choice to reciprocate and move in turn. He opens a door. We have the choice to walk through it (or not).

Sometimes, alternatively, it will just be us stepping out in small ways and initiating based on a word from the Lord (simple actions). Making a phone call, stopping to pray, offering help. It may be simple, but it is a choice to step out in faith. Here's what matters: To walk in God's promises it takes action. Action is only active by choice. Choice powers action. Listen to this definition:

"Receiving or subjected to an action *without* responding or initiating an action in return. / Accepting or submitting without objection or resistance; submissive. / Existing, conducted, or experienced without active or concerted effort."

---

1. Strong, *Strong's Expanded Exhaustive Concordance of the Bible*, 1490.

If your faith "walk" can be described like this, you actually have a faith "sit" because this is the definition of "passive" according to Wordnik.com. Time to get walking. Time to make some choices!

YOU CAN'T OUTRUN YOUR FORK

I once passed a marquee advertising weight loss that read "You can't outrun your fork." While they had intended it to be a witty joke about not being able to avoid eating, I found it incredibly profound. Rather than the utensil, I pictured a fork in the road. You can't outrun your fork. You cannot go through life long without making choices. If you resolve to not choose, you'll end up stuck. Historically, choices come on the scene about the time we do. In the garden of Eden, choice was created with the creation of the tree of life. Once created, it introduced a dangerous love triangle we still tango with to this day. We have the choice to follow God's advice and instructions or to believe the enemy and agree with him.

God's guiding voice is *always* there. If you're unsure if you've heard God, perhaps it is because that voice has become so familiar it blends in to everyday life. Like a GPS, God is at every turn gently guiding the way. Sometimes we have our music blaring so loudly on the drive we forget to listen for the GPS. Though He is speaking, we still have the choice to listen or not. I have, unfortunately, heard many things blamed on "God's will" that sound a whole lot more like a lack of responsibility for bad choices. Sure, God works with it all, and He certainly doesn't plan out an easy path for us, but when we *choose* according to our flesh, we can end up far from God's goal for us.

God longs for us to hear Him. He wants to be an active counselor guiding our choices. So much so that He is not afraid to repeat Himself. I draw so much personal comfort from the fact that God didn't abandon Gideon to silence when he asked for the most absurdly specific formation of dew to be his confirmation, *still* wasn't convinced, and then asked for *another* absurdly specific formation of dew (Judges 6:36–40). Out of my husband and I, I'm the one asking God for one more confirmation even in mid-leap of faith. My husband, on the other hand, will pray, receive his answer, and continue with unwavering resolve. Our patient Father knows what we need and knows how to speak to us in ways that *we specifically* will hear. So, if you're afraid of "missing it," don't be. In the gospels, Jesus talks to His disciples about the prophecies about His death and resurrection over and over, yet somehow has the patience to let Thomas examine His scars. We know because Jesus "is the same yesterday, today, forever" (Hebrews 13:8) that today He will *still* repeat His messages. When the Lord has something to say, He doesn't just hope you catch it the first time. His messages are persistent, but we do need to listen.

CHOOSING GOD & BEING CHOSEN

God chose us first. But He still longs for us to choose Him. The key to finding what you are chosen *for* starts with choosing God first. The word for this is seek. Over eighty-five verses in the Bible speak of seeking God. Among those are Proverbs 8:17: "those who diligently seek me will find me" and Jeremiah 29:13 "you will seek Me and find Me when you seek Me with all your heart." Seek is synonymous with "to look for, to be on the lookout for, to hunt for, to be in quest of, to work toward, to call for, or to beg for" (according to Merriam Webster). This paints a picture that is not merely an openness to encountering God. This is a hungry, passionate, all-out quest. This kind of seeking stays up late or gets up early, asks persistently until there is an answer, and does not give up when the seeking gets tough.

Jesus describes the Father's heart toward us seeking Him in a parable about a widow (Luke 18:1–8). She had not received justice and kept bugging the local judge. While it says nothing of *how* she did this, I like to picture her loitering outside the judge's home, sending him message after message, and talking to everyone he knows to find out how to get through to him. She may have learned his routine, learned when and where she would be most likely to find him, learned what he liked to try to entice him to take her case, and used every bit of persuasion she could in shameless audacity to seek his answer. This likely altered almost all of this widow's choices. It changed where she chose to be at any given time, who she chose to speak to, or even what she chose to buy or not buy. Now swap the widow and judge for you and God. Are you seeking God in such a way that is changes where you choose to be? Who you choose to speak to? What you choose to buy or not buy? Our seeking should change our choices if we are seeking with all our heart, soul, mind, and strength.

HIDE AND SEEK

Seeking God can carry with it the misconception that God is trying to allude us or hide from us. In my experience, this is not the case. While God wants us to seek Him, He longs to be found by us and delights in sharing with His children. I picture playing hide and seek with my children. Do I play because I'm being mean to them or alluding them? Do I not want to be found by them? Quite the opposite, actually. We play because it's fun and because it invents a joy-loaded context for discovery. It's like our human tradition of "hiding" a gift in gift wrapping. With both hide and seek or opening gifts the *best* part (for us and most definitely for the Lord) is being *found*. He's not trying to deceive us. That's the enemy. He's trying to multiply our joy.

He tells us to *seek*. He *wants* us to loiter at His metaphorical door in prayer, waiting for what He would say. He wants us to scour the word, looking for how we may find Him. He wants us to send up prayer after prayer and then relentlessly look for His answers. He will never turn away a seeking heart. He promises that in Jeremiah 29:13: "If we seek Him, we *will* find Him when we seek Him with all our hearts".

To clarify, seeking is an attitude of the heart. It is not a specific set of *what* to do as much as it is a method for *how* to do. Jeremiah 17:10 says that God "searches the heart and examines secret motives." It may be a hundred prayers that bring the breakthrough, or it may be a passionate but short single declaration. It's not the quantity of time we spend seeking the Lord but the quality (although quantity does breed intimacy in much the same way that you are closer to the friends you spend more time getting to know). The heart that seeks must also do so purely. We cannot have the legalistic attitude that if we seek enough that God will grant us our way. God *longs* to give us the desires of our hearts. God also only gives *good* gifts (James 1:17). We can be guaranteed that seeking God will find God as well as have our thirsts satiated, but we cannot bribe or manipulate His answers. Nor would we want to if we were able to attain the understanding of all things as God does.

He always leaves in our hands the power of choice. We can choose to seek His answers and guidance...or not. If your spouse had to do everything you said and had no choice about it, would you feel loved by their obedience? There is something robbed from the gift when it is given under compulsion. Think of if your spouse *had* to make you breakfast versus if your spouse *chose* to make you breakfast. One is a chore. The other is an act of love.

> *"Each of you should give what you have decided in your heart to give, not reluctantly or under compulsion, for God loves a cheerful giver."*
>
> *2 Corinthians 9:7*

God doesn't want to be your chore. He wants to be your *choice*. Many wonder why He even put a Tree of Knowledge of Good and Evil in the garden. I wouldn't doubt that it is for the same reason He inspired 2 Corinthians 9:7; He *wants* to be *chosen*.

> *"You did not choose me, but I chose you"*
>
> *John 15:16a*

He has chosen you time and time again with His relentlessly pursuing love. He will always respect your choices. He created choice! He sits in all of His power, all of His glory, all of His perfection, and He patiently waits, hoping to be *your* choice. He hides his love notes and callings in plain sight and hopes you will seek them. It will be the wildest game of hide and seek of your life.

THE GOODWILL OF FREEWILL

One of the reasons seeking is so important is that God's word is *living*. His guidance updates as our life circumstance update. The world throws many things at us, and staying connected through seeking is the best way to continue navigating it all. The cliché abounds that "God is in control." Well...kind of.

Remember having your driver's permit with your parent in the car? I remember learning to drive in the Trinity University parking lot. My little brother was sweating from the summer heat and literally bored to tears in the back seat, whining to go home. My mother tried to keep a calm tone and put on her best "instructor" voice, even though I could tell from her heavy exhales through rounded lips and repeated whispers to herself under her breath that she was doing all she could to trust her child behind the wheel.

"Alright now slowly accelerate, and we'll do a lap," she instructed. After following her every instruction perfectly, my confidence was soaring. Our practice was about to come to an end, so she told me to begin to feather the brake to slow down and then pull it into a parking space. I mistook the brake for the gas, and an unsuspecting bicyclist whizzed in front of me. Instead of slowing, I did three revs on the gas and floored it.

"*Feather*! *Feather*!!!" My mom screamed. I switched to the brake and screeched the car to a stop. The poor bicyclist started working double time to get out of the way and stared me down like I had three heads as he passed. While my mother could have insisted on never letting me drive, she wanted her child to learn how. This involved surrendering some of that control, even when she was a more qualified, more experienced, safer, and smoother driver. She knew if she did, it would allow me to make my own choices, make mistakes, and, ultimately, get really good at driving. She also didn't leave me alone in the car to figure it out. She was there to walk through it with me.

While God holds all power (1 Chronicles 29:11–12, Job 42:2, Isaiah 14:27) and can intervene, He often *chooses* to rein it in by sharing a portion of this power in giving freewill or *choices*. He is the parent in the passenger seat, guiding us turn by turn, scream-ing "feather!!!" when we are out of control. He could be in control of every choice we ever made, but to do so would mean that we would never learn or grow. Instead, He shares control. Sometimes, He truly reaches over and takes the wheel by shutting a door in life that would be a bad choice. Other times, He lets us make the choice, guiding us from the passenger seat. No wonder we have such a crazy world! Imagine a world full of student drivers. Spiri-tually, that's what we have. But those who listen to the instructor and learn from their training begin to drive how He drives and become more and more trustworthy on the road of life. I want to be a child of God who doesn't make Him clutch the arm rests with white knuckles and grind His teeth but the child that He trusts enough to recline the seat and kick His feet up on the dash.

THE WAITING ROOM VS. THE BOARD ROOM

In the driving analogy, some of us are parked with Jesus. We're wondering when things are going to get going while He patiently waits for *us* to just start the engine. When we are procrastinating or stuck in the paralysis of indecision, it can be likened to taking a seat in a waiting room instead of the board room. We are sitting anxiously in a "waiting room" of life, waiting for what will happen to us next, waiting for news, waiting on a person, waiting on a paycheck (or lottery win) . . . essentially passing the time until the next "thing" happens to us. What we don't realize is that we weren't made to sit in Heaven's waiting room, waiting for the next decision rendered. We're actually seated in what's way closer to Heaven's board room. While God doesn't need our permission or power, He lovingly wants our input, gives us opportunity for partnership, and coaches our "motions." He wants our choices. When we just sit there inactive, it turns into a spiritual game of Tetris.

Tetris used to be my favorite pastime between college classes (in the days before "apps" were a thing). In a game of Tetris, as each piece is dropped into view one at time, and that's your cue to rotate that piece to fit most effectively into the existing pieces, "clear" lines, and, ultimately, advance levels. When you just sit there, the pieces still drop. They begin to stack up high, and the game is quickly lost. I picture this a lot like how some of us do life. New pieces come at us from God, and He's excitedly waiting for us to see how they fit and to listen to His coaching for how to work them all together. When we just sit there hoping God will drop everything perfectly into place with absolutely no interaction on our part, we are letting our chances pile up into a cluttered mess that's actually difficult to sort through. Yes, God does bless us and just drop blessings into our laps sometimes, but He certainly doesn't do so for those blessings to just sit there. There are always choices about how we can utilize, flip, turn, spin, and put to work the things the Lord is lining up.

DRIVING WITH THE EMERGENCY BRAKE

I learned to drive on an old maroon Camry. I rarely got in as a teenager without being in a hurry. Rushing to school, rushing to work, or not wanting to be left out of an impromptu friend gathering, my keys were never far from the ignition. I would jump in the car, fumble for the right key from amidst the attached slew of tacky keychains acquired from friends, trips, crafts, and memories before flying out of the driveway. Except when I didn't. Countless times I would slowly creep backwards as I punched the gas until it dawned on me. *Ugh, emergency brake!* I always put on my emergency brake when parking. My dad had me convinced if I didn't, I would certainly find my car had rolled away and was gone. Remembering to take it off is *still* a struggle. When you're expecting to hit the road and burn some serious rubber, there is nothing worse than feeling slowed down. Whether it's stuck in traffic, a dead-end job, or physically trapped, being stuck sends us on an emotional rollercoaster from panic to hopelessness and everywhere in between.

There are those times in which we have such a clear idea and plan of what we *think* will succeed or that thing that "if we just had ____ everything would line up." The Israelites ended up stuck circling the same mountain for forty years because they had all sorts of ideas of how they could do things differently than God told them.

For years in my professional life, I had the pedal to the metal and the emergency brake on. I had been through too much schooling and training in Counseling to not use it. I couldn't change gears now! My inflexibility cost me years in dead-end jobs. I remember one day driving home when the Lord told me, "Leave your job and work for me." Like Peter and the fishermen, how could I keep holding my nets? The allure and heart-pounding dreams of what the Lord could have for me urged me to make the leap. On the other hand, the grinding emergency brake of "what will people think?" "what about my security?" or "what about my plans?" held me back.

When I finally swallowed my pride and took the leap, I dreamed of what fantastic upgrade of a career could just fall into my lap. Turns out the upgrade looked a whole lot more like a downgrade at first. My next season took the form of volunteering for a kids' Bible study, starting a tiny blog, and going on a ten-day mission trip. If I hadn't listened and had gone by appearances, I would have never made the trade. Now, our home is flooded with joy in the form of seventy-five teenagers a week that we have the blessing of leading as youth pastors. That one mission trip turned into a breaking of my heart for the unreached and, ultimately, the catalyst to starting my own humanitarian organization. And the tiny blog? It grew slowly and steadily and much to my anxiety (since I really never enjoy the spotlight or being seen) and eventually evolved into the Arrows of Zion ministry that led me here. Spending a Monday morning writing this piece of this book. Sometimes, despite appearances, if we just get out of our own way and *listen,* we lift the parking brake on our dreams.

WWJD

Back in the nineties, I proudly sported one of the popular WWJD (What Would Jesus Do?) bracelets with rainbow-striped fabric and widely-stitched black letters. While the sentiment was a great one (reflecting on Christian character before making decisions) it fed into my old, legalistic thinking in a dangerous way. What was the "right" answer to my specific day-to-day decisions? For many decisions there was no scenario in the Bible that *exactly* fit. It was more of a haphazard guess each time, and for a rule follower, I was feared that maybe I was getting it wrong.

My middle name means "God has shown grace." Boy, has He ever! If anything, that bracelet showed me I couldn't be Jesus. Not even close. We all know that, but I think it takes at least one failure on a catastrophic level to truly drive it home. I had to learn, like we all do, what grace even was. Grace means, on a foundational level, *without earning it*. Without having followed every rule perfectly, with our mistakes and messes and failures, we are *still* forgiven, chosen, and blessed. We are still loved, and we are given favor and opportunity beyond what we could ever earn. How do we make choices like Jesus? The answer is not *only* a set of instructions but an *attitude of the heart*.

> "Jesus Replied, 'Lord the Lord your God with all your heart and with all your soul and with all your mind. This is the first and greatest commandment. And the second is like it: 'Love your neighbor as yourself.' All the Law and the Prophets hang on these two commandments."
>
> Matthew 22:37–40

All of the law and prophets hang on these two commandments. Wow. That last section of the verse often seems to trail off into a mumble, but in my opinion, it is the most profound piece of the scripture! It is an easy-to-remember standard to govern our life. Any prophetic word, any law given in the Old Testament, any instruction Paul had for us, any wisdom Solomon had to share, could all be summarized in every effort of our being in the directions of loving God and loving people. This is made to guide every single choice we make. After all, Biblically the law was made and the prophets were sent to help guide *choices*. In those verses in Matthew, Jesus simplifies it without altering it at all. When your sole aim is loving God and loving others, you are doing what Jesus would do. In any choice, this was made to be our compass.

For people like me who enjoy clear expectations and detailed instructions, the renewed mind of the New Covenant is more of a challenge. There is no checklist that ensures us God's approval. We already have it. There are also very real expectations God has of us. Dismissal from *earning* our salvation did not release us from a relationship with God. Relationships have real expectations. You have expectations for your children. You expect your spouse to return your phone calls or say "I love you." These expectations don't add to or take away from your love for them. In fact, these expectations exist *because* you care. Your expectations for those you don't care about intimately (strangers in the grocery store) are far less. Because He cares, God has hopes and desires of us. They don't earn His love. Instead, their existence proves His love.

On the flip side, we also don't earn our troubles. There is no checklist that ensures us freedom from troubles in this world. We will have troubles. In fact, walking with God is walking in direct opposition of the giver of trouble in this world, so they can, in many ways, be expected.

> "In fact, everyone who wants to live a godly life in Christ
> Jesus will be persecuted" 2 Tim. 3:12

When faced with choices, we are not to choose the path of least troubles. We are not to try to anticipate our troubles and steer our life according to our perceived path of least resistance. Some of the most admired figures in the faith encountered more trouble than we can relate to, *but there's hope.* The grace that we don't deserve will always fight harder *for* us then our troubles will fight *against* us.

> "For our light and momentary troubles are achieving for us
> an eternal glory that far outweighs them all."
>
> 2 Cor. 4:17

"Blessed is the one who perseveres under trial because, having stood the test, that person will receive the crown of life that the Lord has promised to those who love him."

James 1:12

"I have told you these things, so that in me you may have peace. In this world you will have trouble. But take heart! I have overcome the world."

John 16:33

CHOOSING THE SCENIC ROUTE

In a results-focused world, "process" is a word that is to our soul as nails on a blackboard are to our ears. We cringe at the thought of the journey or the process. We just want to get there. We want results and measurable progress as validation that what we are doing is correct and worthwhile. When the Israelites were fleeing the Egyptians, they were hungry for confirmation. They had seen sign after sign but still had hearts of weak faith, wondering why God would lead them to a dead end. The Rea Sea was before them with an enemy army chasing them in the rear. Of course, we all know the story ended with God parting the sea and giving them yet another wondrous, miraculous confirmation. Actually, being one of the Israelites living this out, however, it would have been a harder leap of faith.

One of my favorite verses is Exodus 13:17: "When Pharaoh let the people go, God did not lead them on the road through Philistine country, *though it was shorter*. For God said, 'If they face war, they might change their minds and return to Egypt'." What!? I get excited every time I read that. We get a glimpse into the mind of God during those loathed times when we wonder where our shortcut is, when things will get better, or if a change is ever coming. We *hear* Romans 8:28, that God works all things for our good, but do we ever think that maybe He really does do everything for our good?

Maybe God would love to take the shortcut even more than we would, but He knows that in taking it, all the strengthening the process will accomplish would be circumvented, and we would fail to arrive at our promised land. Sometimes, for good reason, God chooses the scenic route. In these times, our power over our situation again lies in a choice. *Choosing* to trust. It takes bravery to follow God through the scenic route. A person's mind looks at a dead end like the Red Sea and calls it quits. A renewed mind calls it possible.

The gospels chronicle the temptation of Jesus. After this amazing beginning to His ministry in which the Holy Spirit comes and anoints Him with power for all He will need to do, He then has His faith tested. Each of the three tests are temptations of *shortcuts*. Knowing Jesus was hungry, he offered a shortcut through His fast (Matthew 4:3). I know I have been hangry enough waiting for a meal before that I could do things that I would not be proud to publish in this book. Jesus *chooses* to trust God to satisfy Him.

Then the enemy offered a shortcut to the miraculous reveal that Jesus was the Son of God by tempting Him to put Himself in harm's way to watch Heaven move to save Him (v. 6). You know that feeling when you do something great and someone else gets the credit for it? Jesus's life was flooded with humility in situations that any of the rest of us would have screamed, "I am the Son of God! I don't have to deal with this!" The enemy knew how much greatness in that man was reined in by divine humility. He dangles the bait of recognition and feeling important under Jesus's nose. Jesus *chooses* not to test God.

Next, the enemy offers a shortcut to power and rule, tempting Him to forego the cross and have all kingdoms of earth just handed to Him (v. 8). At the time all the religious leaders expected the Messiah to be a literal king bringing earthly peace and protection to their people, so becoming the ruler of kingdoms would be conforming to what people wanted Him to be. Haven't we all be attacked like this? Hearing the sly whisper of "if you did that, people would love and approve of you. You'd be exactly what they want you to be. You would *please* people." Not to mention the wealth being a ruler would bring. Jesus was purposefully not born into a wealthy family, and while his wandering, austere lifestyle kept all of His needs met by God, He wasn't stacking up security in piles of gold or silver. Comfort or security are dangerous temptations when they shortcut our reliance on God. The enemy's offer came with the price of worshipping him. Jesus *chooses* to only worship God.

Jesus's response to each of these tempting shortcuts was to recall God's previous words. In other words, He checked His spiritual "map" for the path God had already carved out for Him and stuck to the original route. *He chose the scenic route.* He knew He would get fed again. He knew He would eventually be recognized for who He was by many people. He knew going through the cross would win back the hearts of the people—not just control of them. So, He chose the scenic route to all of these things. When Matthew 4 opens, it says that Jesus "was led into the wilderness by the Spirit." This means God led Him to go, *and Jesus chose to go.* It was during the solitude and desperation that He was tempted with a shortcut. The enemy has not changed his strategies. He targets us to tap out when we also are alone, hungry, and desperate.

Many of us go through seasons in the wilderness with the tempter, and we are often times not privy to how long these seasons will last. These are when the shortcuts become most tempting. We do not know how long we will be in the wilderness. It seems there's no hope in sight. It could all be over if we just took back some of the control. Notice with every temptation that the enemy suggests manipulating God. Abusing His promises to get our way, circumventing His sovereignty in our life, boxing Him into our timelines or demands. I visualize the Father's approving smile and the angels' pure joy and celebration as Jesus willingly chooses the scenic route, no matter how long it takes. The renewed mind chooses the scenic route. The result (v. 11) is that after His third refusal, the enemy left, and He was attended to and refreshed by the angels.

If you are in a place right now where you are following God down the scenic route, keep going. Keep choosing Him, for it is in your power to choose. Your heart may be yearning for the break-through, and you can see no end in sight with your human mind, but your Father smiles and sends deliverance and refreshment the second you choose to pass up the shortcuts of temptation. Just like rolling a heavy stone, the first pushes are the slowest. As you gather momentum, you begin to move faster and faster, but *big things of-ten take time to get moving*. Because just like the Israelites, God always has a reason for leading you around the long way, and His reasons are always to see us flourish and be fulfilled.

A WRONG TURN

Sin is the dark side of this superpower of choice. Sin is any choices that take us in the opposite direction God is calling us. When you ignore the GPS instructions, you'll encounter a warning message of "take a legal U Turn when possible." Throughout the Bible God warns His people time and time again, and those warnings remain. God does not trick or trap. He does not stay silent while we walk off course and then say "Oh, sorry! Since you didn't figure it out, you missed out on your destiny." While the GPS cannot make you turn around, it will keep reminding you and rerouting your course back the opposite direction until you turn.

Sometimes these turns of sin are obvious, like when we fall into hating someone or holding a bitter grudge. Other times they are more insidious, like when Jonah chose to sail in the opposite direction of the dangerous city of Nineveh to which God called him. He just chose a different destination for his vacation. Doesn't seem so bad. But he *knew* God needed him elsewhere and turned the opposite direction.

Sin. A decided turning away. In steering clear of sin, it's less about focusing on going about life not doing "bad" things. In fact, sometimes we get so caught up in what *not* to do that we forget that God has bigger dreams for us than just staying out of trouble. Steering clear of sin is far more of a focused and persistent effort to do what God is telling you to do. We can trust that, despite His sometime-unorthodox ways, God will never tell us to contradict

His word. What He asks of us will always be Kingdom-focused and embody loving Him and loving others. The task for us is to know Him and His character enough to discern His voice from all the others that clamor for our attention. As God renews our minds, He tunes them to hear His voice, and that voice becomes a coach for all of our choices.

In our youth group we play a game that paints the perfect spiritual picture of this. The kids are broken up into partners. One partner is blindfolded while the other is the "coach" on the sidelines guiding them through obstacles. The trick is, everyone is going at the same time. You have to know your partner's voice to know what directions to follow. If you start listening to another voice or the coaching for someone else, it won't work. We, also, walk by faith and not sight. We need to know the voice of our Coach and Father. We need to discern it well enough to distinguish it from the world, the enemy, and even our own flesh. We also need to know when a word is for us or for someone else. Just like instruments can be tuned and then, if left sitting or if conditions change, need to be re-tuned, we are constantly re-tuning our ears to God's voice.

> *My sheep listen to my voice; I know them, and they follow me. John 10:27*

TAKE IT TO GOD:

Ask each of these questions one at a time, and wait in the still silence for God's answer. Jot it down!

What is something I can do to take a step of faith towards a promise you have for me?

How can I seek you in such a way that it changes my daily choices?

What is a choice You've been waiting for me to make?

How can I get out of the waiting room and into the board room?

In what ways do I have the emergency brake on?

Highlight a place in my life in which you've taken me on the scenic route, and help me to see it through Your eyes.

Chapter Three

222

"In a large house there are articles not only of gold and silver, but also of wood and clay; some are for special purposes and some for common use. Those who cleanse themselves from the latter will be instruments for special purposes, made holy, useful to the Master and prepared to do any good work."

2 TIMOTHY 2:20–21

222

I CLICK MY PHONE to check the time. It's 2:22. I squint against the bright Texas sun as I walk to my car. I have a missed call from a number I don't recognize, the first three digits of which are 222. The car's license plate next to me glints in the sun, highlighting the last three characters: 222. I start the car, and it picks back up in the song right where it had left off, at 2 minutes and 22 seconds in. The average MPG for the fuel economy display shows 22.2 miles per gallon. After a full *two* days where those numbers continued to resurface again and again, I was riding in the back of a Suburban with a large group of family members. I glance at the clock, and it's 2:22 again. I start to wonder if maybe this is growing from a coincidence to a God-incidence.

When I see a certain number over and over like this, sometimes the numbers correspond to a verse. Sometimes it draws attention to where in the Bible that number shows up. Sometimes it's something else entirely. There is no precise methodology of decoding God's messages, and to create one would be akin to creating another Levitical law. It would miss the point (of knowing God's heart) entirely. One thing is certain. God says "If you seek me, you will find me if you seek me with all your heart" (Jeremiah 29:13). If you start looking, you will eventually have the answer revealed to you, though it may even take a long time. God would not send us a message we could never find the meaning of. That would be as pointless as me trying to have a conversation with my husband in a language he doesn't speak. When He gets our attention with something, He wants to intrigue us enough for us to want to ask Him what it means. He loves when we *want* desperately to know what He is saying. He is *excited* to answer us. "Call to me and I will answer you" (Jeremiah 33:3), "ask me for anything" (John 14:14), "ask me" (Psalm 2:8), "ask and it will be given to you, seek and you will find" (Matthew 7:7), "if any of you lacks wisdom, let him ask of God" (James 1:5). Sensing a theme? You will know when you find what God's trying to show you. It's the "aha!" moment. He *knows* our hearts, and He speaks to them in ways we can understand.

When I first began tentatively stepping into conversation with God about writing this book, I kept feeling drawn to a particular Bible verse because it spoke of how when we clear out the things in us for common purposes, we become things for special use. Uncommon vessels are things for special use. Not being as good as I would like to be with Biblical addresses, I had to look up the verse to remember where in the Bible it was located. 2 Timothy 2:20–21. The first three numbers of the verse are 222. Go figure. It was like an inside joke with God. I literally laughed in disbelief when I saw it. A little holy wink from God that said "oh yeah, My fingerprints are all over this." God keeps going until He gets our attention.

DREAM INTERPRETATION

On a sunny morning, I climbed in the car, my mind still fixed on figuring out the meaning of my dream the night before. It had been the third one in a series of reoccurring dreams over the course of a year, so I knew it must mean something. Though each dream was slightly different, in each one I was awakened from a sleep or unexpectedly pulled into another room and told that I needed to get dressed right away for the play. I would always ask for my lines, and I never got an answer. Finally, frustrated, I would ask "Can someone just tell me what part I'm playing at least?" They would always respond that I was playing the lead. Though thrown into the process at the last minute, I would spend the rest of the dream excitedly getting ready to go on stage.

"Grab your passport and my hand..." sang Taylor Swift through the speakers of our old Suburban as I drove down the street. I slow to a stop at the next red light, and stopped dead across from me at the intersection in a giant RV with the word "PASS-PORT" in huge letters. God had been tugging on my heart for some time about taking a leap of faith and joining a mission trip to Nicaragua. This is the same mission trip mentioned in the last chapter which ended up being quite a powerful jumping off point in my life. I didn't know that yet. My first step to going was renewing my passport. After the slew of attacks on our finances, I cringed at how I would even come up with the passport money-much less over two thousand dollars to go to Nicaragua! Isn't that how the enemy works? Attacks to the pocketbook right at the time of an important investment or opportunity to give have almost become a welcomed challenge and confirmation. I heard the call, but that time I decided to wait. I got the papers, even filled them out, and set them on my nightstand as I prayed for one more confirmation.

Less than a week later, sitting at church with my husband, I fixed my wide-eyed gaze on a man I had never met before. I watched, almost in surreal slow motion, as he said "I don't know what this means, but I feel like God wanted me to tell you to get your passport." Shocked tears stung my eyes, and I laughed. My husband, having heard about God's earlier messages, squeezed my leg. Needless to say, I sent in my passport application the next day. Ironically (or not ironically at all), after taking that step of obedience, the next day I got a text about meetings from a local number I didn't recognize. I assumed it was a wrong number. When I finally asked what the meetings were for, chills ran up and down my back. Nicaragua. Because of *one* mistyped letter in my email address, I had missed out on a couple months of communications about the trip. Miraculously (in true God fashion), the second I took my first leap of faith, the error was spotted and communication opened. I believe that when we step out in faith that God meets us. I stepped out in faith, responding to His words, and mailed off my passport. The *next day* I had communication restored between myself and the Nicaragua team.

As the evening of the first meeting rolled around, I expected the hundred-person group I had seen at the information session months ago. I had stepped out in faith, but I had probably a mustard seed's worth, so my plan was to go and sit in the back. Even though I knew God wanted me to go, I had two thousand dollars to come up with and no idea how in four months I could be on a plane. I walk into the room. There are no chairs. There are only six or eight people gathered around talking. There went my plan of going unnoticed.

As we began to practice, the leader smiled at me and said, "Ok, I need you to play the lead." Warmth flooded my face as I smiled and tried to hide the confusion on my face. Lead? Wasn't a mission trip where you built houses or helped orphanages? Much to my surprise, I learned one of the outreaches planned was going to be a gospel-based skit done in the streets. Then my smile turned very serious as I remembered—the dream! Thrown in at the last minute, playing the lead...it was all so that when I arrived at this moment that I would know that God had seen and planned this for me before I ever got here. The God who stages what we see can orchestrate dreams and recurrences simply so that *when they manifest, we notice.* It's God's equivalents of dog-earring a page or highlighting a sentence. It says, "Pay attention to this! This is important!"

PIZZA, DANIEL, OR SPIRITUAL WARFARE

I've had requests to write about dream interpretation, but the honest truth is dreams are simple. There are three types of dreams: dreams from God, dreams from the enemy, and pizza dreams. Pizza dreams are those dreams that leave you scratching you head, that sound nothing like anything else you're getting from God at the time, and, likely, are not meant to be held to tightly. Just like some thoughts are just our flesh, some dreams are just our mind reacting to half a bag of Cheetos before bed.

Dreams from the enemy are easy to spot because they involve deep fear or dread, and they are usually in the opposite direction of the current words we are getting from the Lord. Their sole purpose is to camouflage as a message from God and get you derailed from your destiny. Our Daniel (or Joseph, or Jacob) moments in which we have dreams from the Lord are sweet treasures. When you have a dream you think may be from the Lord, write it down in as much detail as you can. Then ask yourself these questions:

- How did I feel in the dream? What does that tell me?

- What symbols were in the dream? What do they mean to me? Where (if anywhere) do they show up in the Bible?

- Is this a dream that's literal or figurative?

- What pieces of this sound like God, and, if so, what Biblical instances of God does it remind me of?

- What other confirmations in waking life or dreams have I received that relate to this?

- What could God want to tell me through this dream?

Once you've explored these questions, put a pin in it. Continue living. Engage with God in your quiet time. Notice God throughout your day. If He brings some of these answers to mind, revisit it. Biblically, instances of dreams tell us that God uses them to have special spiritual encounters, confirm direction, or give us glimpses of our callings. Where does your dream fit among those?

Ultimately, dream interpretation goes back to the fact that God will not communicate with us through an unsolvable puzzle. I may not have known what that particular dream meant for a little bit, but, ultimately, I figured it out. God is speaking *to you*, so He will make it understandable *to you*. When you're stumped, pray and ask for more clarity, and God will be faithful to send some in a way that you will understand (*if* it is a dream from Him that needs to be understood). Always trust God more than the dream. Just like Joseph's dreams, often times they aren't literal, and how they play out in real life may not be immediately obvious. Trust the process, and trust that God won't give you a sneak peek or a message that wasn't for good or for your assistance.

THE BIRDS AND THE (BUMBLE)BEES

God speaks in so many ways that it truly could be its own library. The Bible alone is sixty-six books on how God speaks. God has endless creativity. After all, He is the creator. Even the disciples trying to describe Jesus said, "Jesus did many other things as well. If every one of them were written down, I suppose that even the whole world would not have room for the books that would be written" (John 21:25). There is no exhaustive list. Maybe a cardinal shows up on your fence post for a month straight. Maybe radio in the car becomes like Bumblebee from the *Transformers* movies and seems to have the perfect lyrics to speak to your heart. Maybe the word "restore" keeps showing up everywhere. Maybe a certain person keeps crossing your path. These are things any person, regardless of having faith or not, would notice. The difference that brings a renewed mind is saying, "Ok God, I notice this. Now what do I do?" It could be a call to prayer, a call to action, a message about what God is doing in your life, God revealing more of His wisdom and heart to you, or it may not be from God at all.

Either way, taking it to the Lord will answer the question of what to do next.

In 1 Kings 19, Elijah the prophet was desperately seeking God's guidance on facing those who had killed the other prophets and wanted to kill him. You could say it was an important meeting with the Lord. Elijah went up on the mountain and waited for God to speak. A violent wind came, shattering mountains. Elijah still waited. An earthquake shook the ground. Elijah waited still. A fire started after the earthquake, and Elijah still waited. Then a subtle whisper came, and it says "when Elijah heard it, he pulled his cloak over his face and went out and stood at the mouth of the cave," and the Lord began to speak! I get goosebumps when I read that. It may seem strange to include all of those details in the story. Why not just say that Elijah went up on the mountain and spoke with God and cut straight to the meat? I believe the answer is that there is just as much to be learned in this Scripture from *not* hearing God as there is from hearing God.

Elijah was a man who was intimately acquainted with God. In a time of stubborn, hostile, and rebellious people, He stuck close enough to the Lord as His friend to become one of the most famous mouthpieces of the Lord. Just as any of our best friends would recognize our car pulling into the parking lot or recognize our voice calling and move to respond, Elijah recognized His best friend, the Lord. It says something profound that Elijah was not even phased by the wind or earthquake or fire. This man who carried countless (probably many more than were recorded) messages for the Lord *knew* God was about to speak when he heard the *whisper*. The little voice planted in our hearts and heads that pulls us to hope, nudges us when we're headed down the wrong path, and whispers realizations so profound that even though they are dropped into our minds, we know they cannot be created by us. If you are looking for the big and dramatic, like a booming audible voice or bolt of lightning, you may get it. There are times when God speaks like this to people. Much *more* often, however, you will be looking for the wrong thing. It is the barely-perceptible whisper that makes your heart race and your arm hair stand up. This is the voice of God. Our challenge is not to bolt off after the earthquake, thinking we have our revelation. Linger for the whisper.

THE BULLY

In elementary school whenever a kid was teased by a bully, the advice I heard teachers give many times is to ignore the bully. Knowing the bully just wanted to get a rise out of the victim, showing the bully that he or she was not successfully getting to the victim removed all power and, subsequently, all fun from picking on anyone. The enemy is not much different from a bully. He wants to see his power working. He wants to watch as he "wins" by making us feel bad about ourselves or give up our efforts. When we ignore his words and uproot his weeds of negative thoughts, he no longer has power over our mind. It does not mean he will leave us alone. After all, we are his biggest threat. We will, however, become no more mindful of his threats than the buzzing of a gnat. We will have the stability and clarity of a mind fixed on our identity, destiny, and the goodness God has for us. We choose what words we agree with. We tend the gardens of our minds and hearts. We pick what stays and what goes. Time to do some weeding. You've got to make room for all God is going to grow in your life!

While God sows many beautiful seeds of His wisdom in our minds, the enemy is right behind Him sowing weeds. Just as in the Garden of Eden, however, we are the caretakers of the garden. We choose what we uproot and what we water. Many have chosen to uproot the words of the Lord and toss it away as nonsense, silly, childish dreams, or even our own voice. Some continue to water the lies of the enemy until they are fully-flowering bushes of self-hate, anxiety, or self-reliance.

God describes this in Matthew 13 in the Parable of the Sower. The farmer (God) scatters His seeds (His words to us). It says some, due to lack of understanding, have it immediately snatched up by the enemy. Are these people just less intelligent? Does God give understanding to some and to these others who don't understand it's tough luck? Not at all. Jesus says,

> *"You are permitted to understand the secrets of the Kingdom of God. But I use parables to teach the others so that the Scriptures might be fulfilled, 'When they look, they won't really see. When they hear, they won't fully understand.'"*

Luke 8:10

I believe this has less to do with individual differences and a whole lot more to do with *seeking*. Sometimes God is very clear and direct in His messages. Other times He chooses a more symbolic route. Maybe He gives us a dream or a vague prophetic word. Instantly, we may not understand, *but* if we agree with him when the enemy whispers "that makes no sense," "you can't understand that," "you're making that up," or "pay no attention to that," we let our seeds be eaten. We never know what could have sprouted from them.

The sower parable also says that others may get it immediately. They may hear God's words, know exactly what He wants them to do, and accept it. Let's say the church sermon really speaks to your heart. It's about forgiveness, and you *know* it was meant for you. God has been gently nudging you to forgive someone in your life, and you're excited to do so. You bounce your knee in the pew, eager to get out and put it into action. You get out of church and head to lunch. Amidst the din of chattering people and the rush of servers and their trays, you start to come back to the "real world." Though this world is definitely not more real than the spirit world, what we see can definitely *feel* more immediate and real than what is unseen. By the end of the day, you have totally forgotten about the sermon and have done nothing to put it into action. These are those in whom the seeds fall on good soil, but because there is no *root* (and roots take time) it was scorched by the sun of the day and withers and dies. It's the thing the precedes the sprouting. It's the calling or urge that in the time from receiving it and it coming to fruition, there is a great risk of forgetfulness or getting sidetracked preventing roots from being established. Roots are difficult to grow because, much like in the natural, the growth of roots is unseen. You may be praying about something God has put on your heart.

To the outside world, nothing has changed and no one may even know the calling about to spring to life that's been seeded in your heart. In the unseen, however, continuing to remember day after day and taking action in that direction is growing tremendous roots. The results of your persistence will someday poke through the soil.

The sower's seeds are also thrown on a third group of people, those whose seeds sprout but are choked out by weeds and thorns. Maybe we remember what God has promised us, what God has called us to, or what He said to us once upon a time. We let those words grow through our remembrance. I truly lived these words right after our daughter was born. I had gotten plenty of words from the Lord my entire pregnancy that she would be just fine. When she was born, everything seemed normal for the first twenty-four hours. Then, at her infant exam, she was failing the blood oxygen portion. They redid it several times, and the numbers were still alarming. They transferred her to an intensive pod and hooked her up to a heart-breaking number of wires. I was irritated. Not at God, but I was irritated at people. I knew she was fine, and I was ready to go home. *Five long days* wore on, and something happened. Those weeds planted by the enemy slowly grew. What if it's a heart condition? What if it's hypertension? What if she doesn't make it? I kept seeking words, and the words from the Lord never changed. Still, my faith wavered. A weedy mess after those five days, we made our way to the NICU in the closest big city where she was being transferred by ambulance. By this time, we were preparing ourselves to just find out *what* it was. When we made it, the doctors announced she was already out of her cardio tests, and . . . nothing was wrong. She could go home tomorrow.

The relief and joy and praise that washed through us were unlike anything I've ever experienced. But for a full year after that event, the lingering weeds kept cropping up. "What if they missed something?" "What if she doesn't make it?" Over time, I got better at weeding my garden, but not without help from the Lord. It turns out pulling weeds out by the root means healing spiritual trauma. It means releasing them to the Lord instead of trying to take them on, figure them out, or control them ourselves. Handing worries and contingency planning over to the Lord is effectively the *RoundUp* of the spirit world.

That whole traumatic year, I knew what God had said. I also, however, let the lies of the enemy grow. Not only do his lies grow when untended, but they steal all of the nutrients in our lives that were meant to nourish God's words. They suck our energy, our time, our resources and, most importantly, our hope. What happens when we fail to shut down the enemy's responses to those promises is called double-mindedness. Double-mindedness is growing and tending spiritual fruit and spiritual weeds simultaneously. The double-mind is the archenemy of a renewed mind.

DOUBLE TROUBLE

Double-mindedness reminds me of those cartoons where a character has an angel on one shoulder and a devil on the other, both trying to steer him. It is literally allowing two minds to coexist in one body. The one belongs to God. The other belongs to the world and is prime real estate for the enemy or idols to set up shop. James 1:8 says a double-minded man is "unstable in all his ways." It's the constant wavering back and forth. The indecision. The "what if's." The giving in and quitting when the road gets tough.

"How long will you hesitate between two opinions?" lamented Elijah, "If the Lord is God, follow Him; but if Baal, follow him," yet he was met with silence (1 Kings 18:21). That is what straddling a double mind does. It causes hesitation. It renders you without an answer and leaves you stuck. When we are uncertain which way to move, the enemy has us paralyzed in indecision. The paralysis of analysis. "No one can serve two masters," Jesus warns in Matthew 6:24. "You cannot drink the cup of the Lord and the cup of demons" (1 Corinthians 10:21). Your two minds are always going to clash. There is no alignment between God's ways and the enemies, which is why He warns "if anyone loves the world, the love of the Father is not in Him" (1 John 2:15). The fence-sitters and the lukewarm are still loved by God. He *yearns* for them. He rebukes double-mindedness so firmly because He *knows* we cannot fulfill our destinies or be satisfied when we spend our lives in the middle, being guided by two minds, taking a few steps in one direction only to be pulled back a few steps in the other. Like the Israelites wandering in the desert who kept going back and forth from serving God to doubting His power, double-mindedness will leave us circling and circling in the desert, never making it to the promised land. We will be in the same limbo—even after decades—all when it was supposed to only be a forty-day journey.

ASK

If you want to start noticing God's messages and hearing Him more clearly in your life, ask. If you already are intimately acquainted with that familiar inner whisper, ask for more. If you want greater discernment in figuring out the difference between God's voice and the voice of the enemy, ask. There are dozens and dozens of verses on the word ask for a reason! Even the word ask, A-S-K, reminds us to "ask, seek, knock" like Matthew 7:7. In other words, be persistent! Be specific! Be relentless! I am ending this chapter with a prayer that you can feel free to join me in praying. I also invite you to say one of your own. There is no one who says things quite like you, and I would guess, being our Creator, that God loves to hear each of our unique ways to speaking to Him; formal or informal, wordy or brief, silent or aloud. Add your own flavor.

> *God, Speak to me. Speak to me in a way that I will understand. May I laugh at how obvious and surprising the ways You will answer this prayer will be. Thank You that Your answers are already coming. That even as I pray, You are sending Your messages. Open my eyes to signs, wonders, and miracles in my own life. I believe they are there. I silence the enemy in the name of Jesus and pray against any distortions or manipulations or weeds he attempts to sow in Your messages. May You shine light on them to both reveal them for what they are and to help me to weed them out. I pray for eyes to see and ears to hear Your voice. I pray for a greater level of wisdom and discernment to*

know which voice is Yours, mine, and the enemy's. Pull me deeper. Bring me closer. Take me on a clue-finding, treasure-hunting, identity-discovering ride of a lifetime. In Jesus's name, Amen.

TAKE IT TO GOD

Ask each of these questions one at a time, and wait in the still silence for God's answer. Jot it down!

Lord, bring to mind the ways you have spoken to me recently.

What is a new way You want to speak to me?

What are weeds in my thoughts that you want me to pull?

In what ways am I living in double-mindedness?

Lord, I'd like to ask you something specific and seek your response. (take it from here!)

Chapter Four

IS IT SAFE TO GET MY HOPES UP?

"'Did I ask you for a son, my lord?', she said. 'Didn't I tell you, 'Don't raise my hopes'?'"

2 KINGS 4:28

THE HEIGHT OF HOPE

THE LIFE OF A prophet during Biblical times was not exactly the kind that folks would clamor to sign up for. Traveling was long and arduous, crowds were not always receptive, occasionally you would be on the run from those wanting to kill you... It's enough to make the inconvenience of going through TSA security checkpoints at the airport look like a fun day of travel. *Shunem* was a place Elisha traveled multiple times. A local woman reached out with one act of kindness and invited him to dinner. It just goes to show that you never know where one simple act of love can lead. Upon accepting her invitation, Scripture says that from that point on *"whenever* he came by, he stopped there to eat" (2 Kings 4:9). Maybe they became friends, and her true love of generous hospitality made it a joy for her to host him each time. Maybe she sighed and inwardly grumbled each subsequent time she saw him in town thinking "great...I invite this guy once, and now he shows up every time every time." Regardless, we know two things are true. First, that she acted generously in showing him kindness and feeding him each time he was in town. Second, that she truly believed in God and had faith that he was truly God's appointed prophet and not some nutcase or fraud. "She said to her husband, 'I know that this man who often comes our way is a holy man of God'" (2 Kings 4:9). Now, we all know that our spouse gets the most real, unadulterated version of how we're feeling. We may smile and put on a polite face at work, but the deepest truths come out in the comfort of our own homes. If this woman told her husband she believed this man was sent by God, we can safely assume she believed it.

That kind of faith does not go unrewarded—in heaven *or* on earth. Elisha's words to the woman serve as the mouthpiece of God as he calls for her and asks "what can be done for you?" (v. 13). In other words, "what is it that you need or desire?" This is the same question God still whispers to us today. "What is it you need, my faithful one? What do you desire? What do you want Me to do?"

Even when the woman makes no request of Elisha and humbly refuses his offer, Elisha persists and asks those who know her. When they reveal that she has no son (and the assumption is she wanted one...badly), Elisha knows exactly what God wants him to do. Imagine this woman, spending years trying to have a child. The bitter tears of heartbreak in infertility or miscarriages or loss. Since she was a believer, she would have likely prayed about it. Maybe she even wore spots on the floor where she had sunk to her knees in prayer time after time. As years went on, she likely thought God had ignored her prayer. Maybe, being in the Old Testament, she had given up hope, thinking she was under a generational curse or that her infertility was a consequence of some kind of sin. Whatever her process, she did not turn away from God. She did not stop believing in Him or His people, and she did not stop reaching out in kindness to her fellow believers. God had not forgotten her. Her faith, having stood the test of fire, was about to be rewarded in a way that would blow her socks off.

Think of what your answer would be if someone in your church truly asked you, "Is there anything you need or want that

I can give you?" You would likely respond much like she did. "Thanks, but I'm ok." Deeper than that, however, our hungry hearts cry with desires that God wants to use. He is orchestrating just the right timing and needing us to meet Him with a disappointment-proof faith. The fulfillment of them may not looks like what you think, but at their purest, unadulterated form, our desires have a connection to our destinies.

STANDING IN THE DOORWAY

Elisha calls the woman, and it says "she stood in the doorway" (2 Kings 4:15). While this is a minuscule detail, we serve a God who cares about the details, and I find incredible significance in this. Are not the "doorways" in our lives opportunities God gives us and is *calling us through*? Yet all too often we hear the call, come to the doorway, and stand there frozen. We hear God. We respond in a small way, but a lingering timidity keeps us from running through the doorway with expectation. Doorway conversations are brief. Someone talks to you from the doorway when they are passing by your office or when he or she is on their way to the store and wants to see if you need anything. Hovering in the doorway lets you easily cut away from the conversation. God yearns, however, for us to *enter in*.

Elisha tells the woman "About this time next year, you will hold a son in your arms."

She then answers, ""No, my lord! Please, man of God, don't mislead your servant!" (2 Kings 4:16). It does not say she was troubled or distressed. She did not answer Elisha that she didn't *want* a child. She essentially says "don't lie to me." From earlier verses we know she believes Elisha is a holy man! She knows he would not lie. This is the sputtering of a wounded heart that had been let down many times. I envision her face, worn with wrinkle lines from years of worry and heartbreak. With a somber expression and guarded eyes full of sadness, she silently asks, "Is it safe to hope again?"

In a similar season of my life, God (lovingly) called me jaded. I knew the basic connotations, but I looked up the specific definition. Webster defines it as "made dull, apathetic, or cynical by experience or by having or seeing too much of something." Haven't we all been there? These are those times when you've seen your hopes fall through too much, so you get tired. Your hearing gets dull. You stop caring as much. More seriously, you stop hoping. The interesting thing about "jaded" is within that word is "jade." Jade is a soft stone, which is often why it was used to carved. You don't see many carved diamonds for a reason. When we let disappointment jade us, we become impressionable. Instead of being resolute, we let lies sink in and we let ourselves be shaped by our circumstances. My guess is this woman was a little jaded too.

I KNEW IT!

True to His word, a year later she is a doting mother to a son. I love to imagine the surreal joy she felt every time she held that boy. I see her gazing at her child in absolute awe that this God who is *real* really sees her and cares for her desires. Like the rest of us, however, her faith was still being built. In what sounds like every parent's nightmare, one day the child, who had grown, got a headache. He was helping his father with harvesting the fields, so the father had his servant bring him back to his mother at home (2 Kings 4:18–20). Anyone who is a parent knows that feeling of your heart dropping to your stomach when you find out something has happened to your child.

The child sat on his mother's lap, it says, until noon, and then died. *What*?! Can you imagine your miracle dying in your arms? Imagine all the thoughts that must have run through her head. "Was this all for nothing?" "Is God punishing me?" "Could I have prevented this?" The enemy may have been trying his best to tempt her mind, but her actions reveal more about the state of her faith. She lays the boy on the guest bed she had made for Elisha each time her came through town (v 21), and she *doesn't tell her husband.* To the logical mind, this is weird. It even seems wrong.

To her *renewed* mind, though, we can guess that she knew sending word to him was wasted time because of her hope in what God could do. You can almost *feel* her hope. She places enough faith in God's miraculous power that she thinks, "No need to worry my husband *unless* the man of God says he is not going to get well." The modern-day equivalent of this would be calmly saying, "I'll seek the Lord first. If God says it's his time, then I will tell my husband, and we will grieve. If God has a miracle waiting in the wings, I will proceed in faith, wait to spread news of the *testimony*, and won't bother taking the time to spread the word of the *attack*."

She asks her husband for a servant and a donkey to go see Elisha (v. 22). It not being a Sabbath or New Moon, her husband is confused (v. 23). She clearly has the peace of God in her heart, because I am telling you right now, if my son had died, calmly and casually talking to my husband would be a miracle in and of itself. So great was her faith *because*, years earlier, she had experienced first-hand God's miraculous provision, hope beyond hope, and after that, she *knew* that the only thing that mattered was seeking the Lord's guidance.

When she finally reaches Elisha, she had clearly been wrestling with thoughts on the way. Her cool strength now dissolves to a desperate plea, "Did I ask you for a son, my lord? Didn't I tell you 'Don't raise my hopes?'" (v. 28). I can almost feel her anguished tears. Anger and the old wound of disappointment reopened, her words read like, "I knew it! I knew it was too good to be true." In times of trials, that great confidence and bold faith can break down. God is patient with us in these times. Elisha, mirroring the Father's heart, promises not the leave her. When he goes to heal the boy, it isn't instant. He tries and tries, and finally the boy is revived! Again, the woman's desires are fulfilled. Again, the miraculous happens.

Each experience that requires faith in our lives is like building the foundation of God's temple in our hearts. When storms come—which they will—a strong foundation will be untouched by the storm's fury. Is it safe to hope again? The answer is yes. Because we know that God's plans for us are good and that His heart is to prosper us, to give us a future we can hope for, and not to harm us, we know there is *always* something to hope for. Do things always play out the way we expect or the way we would choose? No. But do not give up your faith when trouble comes. If you're not at a happy ending it just means *you're not at the end.* We serve a Lord that works *all things* for good.

Without this renewed-mind perspective, many see the death of dreams or waves of devastating destruction come in their lives, and *we stop.* We do not go to God and ask what can be done (like the woman did). We don't even bother to load the donkey because we see it as the end. We forget that when God promised us miracles and provision and the fulfillment of our heart's desires, that He never promised us a life free of these kinds of storms in between. We forget that those two things don't cancel each other out. Just because there is trouble doesn't mean God doesn't have plans for our hearts' desires. Just because the enemy steals or kills in our lives doesn't mean that the Lord doesn't have a miracle recompense set up ahead. *Both* hope beyond our wildest dreams and strife are true. In fact, He promised that we *would* have troubles just because of the nature of this world. "But take heart!," He says. In other words, *keep your hopes up!* "For I have overcome the world" (John 16:33). In the end God wins. In the end, good happens. *If* we don't stop prematurely.

TO TEST OR NOT TO TEST?

If you are human, you have known disappointment. This impression that not everything hoped for can be gotten is attained as early as the first few years of life. When our daughter was only one she was already throwing fits because she wanted a knife on the counter that she (obviously and for good reason) could not have. My son knows this same disappointment when the turtle he hoped would be immortal passed away. Sometimes, just like the knife, we are kept from our hopes because God knows better than us that it wouldn't be good. In those times we have to trust. Other times, like the turtle, His heart is grieved with ours. These tragedies have a lot more to do with living in a fallen world than the will of the Father.

Still, we are called to hope. We are called to press in. Our hope is a useful tool—like a canteen of water for the journey. What if, like my daughter, we are hoping for the wrong thing? Or what if, like my son, we are hoping for something that is unfortunately a casualty of a fallen world? How do we distinguish what God is calling us to place our precious, fragile hope into? There is no formula or litmus test. There is only one way to know if we're being called to take a leap of faith, or if God is waving His arms telling us "Don't jump off the cliff!!!" The answer is *ask*.

There is a great fear that surrounds testing God in the spiritual community. While it is true that Jesus Himself quotes Deuteronomy 6:16 in saying "Do not put the Lord your God to the test," it is often left out that the sentence ends "as you did in *Massah*." *Massah* was the site at which the Israelites in the desert *rebelled* against the Lord. They did not ask for a sign from God, genuinely seeking His guidance. Rather, they deliberately did the opposite of what had already been shown to them. In fact, each time in the Bible when Jesus sighs despairingly at the Pharisees asking for a sign, He does so because *they are trying not to believe*. Their motive is to prove Him false rather than to prove Him real or to find a legalistic entrapment to give reason to execute Him.

> Then some of the Pharisees and teachers of the law said to him, "Teacher, we want to see a sign from you." He answered, "A wicked and adulterous generation asks for a sign! But none will be given it except the sign of the prophet Jonah.
>
> (Matthew 12:38–39).

Let's remember, though, that the sign of Jonah was when Jonah *had clearly heard God's call to go to Nineveh and decided to disobey*. Even in the literal storm of his disobedience, God *still* sent a whale to swallow him until he decided to change course and do what God had instructed. Friends, God *wants* us to ask for signs when we need confirmation or don't know which way to go.

God doesn't want is for us to make Him prove Himself to us as a condition of believing. God also doesn't want for us to ask *already knowing* what He has said but wanting to force Him into a different answer.

I wonder if Jesus asked aloud in Mark 8:12 why "this generation" always asks for a sign *because* He was dumbfounded that after all the signs over decades and centuries that the Lord had given, they *still* wanted more signs. Perhaps they were "sign shopping" and looking for Him to do or say something more palatable for them. We should not *require* of God that He prove Himself . . . we should *inquire* of God to prove ourselves. Ask God. Then prove your faith by acting and believing in accordance with the answers He sends.

Gideon, mentioned earlier, is a perfect example of an earnest heart simply seeking to be doubly sure that he knows what God is saying. Gideon in Judges 6:36–40 comes up with a crazy test, asking God to send him a sign confirming that God will save Israel through Gideon. *God honors his request for a sign twice.* Gideon was not more special that you. In fact, we have an impartial God who knows you are just as special as any of the chosen ones in the Bible (Romans 2:11).

Still not convinced you can ask for a sign? God invites us specifically to watch for signs of confirmation and blessing when we tithe.

> *"Bring the whole tithe into the storehouse, that there may be food in my house. Test me in this,"* says the Lord Almighty, *"and see if I will not throw open the floodgates of heaven and pour out so much blessing that there will not be room enough to store it."*
>
> *Malachi 3:10*

When God gives us a word or direction, it is a good one. His word is solid, and He knows it. In fact, He is excited for you to see how solidly trustworthy His word is. He invites us to first ask His direction and then test Him by taking Him at His word and seeing the beauty that follows when we obey!

SIMON SAYS

Remember the old playground game *Simon Says*? The key to winning was to only follow the instructions that "Simon said". If you acted on something that wasn't what Simon said, you had to go back and start at the beginning. It can be a lot like that when stepping out in faith. Before we step out, we must ask ourselves, "did God say?". Is this something that just *seems* like a good leap of faith to take? Is this just the next logical step? Or is this actually a calling to step out in faith? When asking if it safe to hope and step out in faith, that question is always answered with another question; Did God say?

Moses knew this all too well. His words have become my heart cry, and if I had to sum up my whole spiritual life in one verse, this would be it:

> "Then Moses said to him, "If your Presence does not go with us, do not send us up from here." Exodus 33:15

Like the scene that stings your eyes with tears at the end of a romantic movie, Moses passionately declares that he doesn't ever want to be where God is not. He will only go where God goes. If God does not send him and go with him, he wants no part of it. This coming from the man who remained steadfast even in the wilderness when the rest of the Israelites disobeyed. He knew that God's command was the x factor. The game changer.

Elijah knew this too. He set up a holy duel between God and the secular idol Baal of the time. Now, I don't know if you're like me, but when it comes to giant leaps of faith, I would prefer my test to be alone with God rather than in front of hundreds and hundreds of people. Talk about pressure! But our God meets us in the middle. The greater we step out *in the direction He commands*, the greater and more spectacular of a display He makes in meeting us there.

The task for the duel was simple. Whoever's god could light the wood for the sacrifice would be proven to be the true god. Baal's prophets called out and danced...nothing. Elijah's confidence grew, and he starts some trash-talking from the sidelines. Sarcastically he says "Perhaps he is deep in thought or busy or traveling. Maybe he is sleeping..." (1 Kings 18:27). Nothing works. Turns out Baal isn't the one true living God and is unable to light the fire. Now, God is up. To raise the stakes even more, Elijah commanded that the wood for his offering be doused with water—not once—but three times. *He prayed specifically saying that he had "done all these things at [God's] command"* (v. 36), and *flame on*! Elijah followed God's commands. Elijah asked for a sign. Elijah is confirmed, and God is glorified. Only because God was at the steering wheel of that leap of faith. Not sure where to go? Look before you leap. Look to God before making a leap of faith, and make your heart's cry like Moses, saying "I will not go without you!"

DESIRE: FRIEND OR FOE?

Desire is a word that has starkly divided the Christian community. To some desire is a dark and forbidden fruit of the fleshly side that is to be submitted and quenched as a sacrifice to God. To others desires are God-given cravings serving as a promise of what is to come and usually become the ground on which we come with our Scripture-wielding demands that God satisfy what He put in us. The truth is more likely somewhere in the middle. In looking at Scripture, we are warned to steer away from "foolish and harmful desires" (1 Tim 6:9) yet commanded to "desire earnestly spiritual gifts" (1 Corinthians 14:1).

That alone tells us that desire is not a bad thing. We are supposed to desire and, more than that, to desire *earnestly.* Earnestly is defined by Merriam-Webster as being "serious and intent; a considerable or impressive degree or amount." We are to desire things so much that it is impressive or noteworthy! It is *what* we desire, however, that is important. Most desires come from parts of us that were designed strategically by God. Those desires can be misdirected, but at their most original root they are the fabric of our role in the great story God writes with our life. When you are battling with desires and wondering if they are from God, try asking God to show you His *original design* for these desires. If you desire love, ask God how *He* plans to fill that desire and what *He* planned to do. If you desire adventure, ask God to open doors to the adventures *He* has planned for you and to open your eyes to see them. Insert whatever you desire and ask God to reveal what that desire was supposed to be for and how you can honor Him with it. There is nothing more powerful than bringing glory to God in a way that you love so much that you can't get enough of it!

LETTING THE CREATOR BE CREATIVE

Desires can also become the root of bitterness. When our desires go unfulfilled, they become sore spots. We have preconceived expectations about when and how God is going to fulfill His promises. When unmet, these expectations can make it appear that God isn't planning to show up. In a quick mental review of all Biblical stories you can recollect, in how many does God show up in the way or timing that those individuals expected? By my count, the answer is not many. Unless God has given you a very specific revelation and it comes to pass, we can assume that God understands the moving pieces of the universe and choices and consequences in a way that is literally too massively complex for our human understanding.

Hearing that God would fulfill His promises but potentially in a way that looks differently than expected used to make my stomach sink. The deeper I've walked with the Lord, though, I realize He's not the God of "knock offs" or "less than." Him fulfilling desires in a way that we don't expect can only *outdo* our expectations and *better* fulfill our needs. You may be in a place where you think of God as the type of Father who if you asked for a car would give you a *Hot Wheels*. In fact, God is a God who, when asked for a *Hot Wheels* would give you a real car. He is the God of giving abundantly more than we can ask for or imagine! By definition this means that we cannot imagine the things He wants to give us. It's natural then that sometimes God takes an unexpected road in fulfilling our heart's desires! It's because He is doing more than we can imagine and giving more extravagantly than we could ask for.

I like to imagine God's plans for our lives being similar to those navigation apps for phones that contain information about traffic and wrecks along the way. Based on developments taking place in areas of the road we cannot see from where we are, the time to the destination may change or the application will even reroute to avoid a wreck or dead end. If we did not have the information as to "why," we would become distressed at our phones wondering why our estimated arrival time changed from ten minutes to twenty-eight minutes, or wondering why the directions are now telling us to take what seems to be a longer route. When we know that more time is added to our route because of construction on the road or that we are being rerouted because of a wreck, while it doesn't make waiting more fun, we are better able to accept the information being given to us. Sometimes God knows about spiritual short cuts or is having to do some rerouting due to sin or the enemy, so it looks to our natural eye like we're taking the long way—or worse—that we will never arrive. He is trying to help us get to where we want to be! He wants us in the center of His will doing all He created for us to do, which will be the most fulfilling place for us too! Sometimes the route to the fulfillment of those desires isn't what we expect. We just don't always have the advantage of knowing the "whys." When we trust our Navigation (God), we can trust the route. We can also trust that the *destinations* along the way are going to delight us (even if some of the obstacles on the road are not fun at the time).

We fall into hopelessness when we try to micromanage how God blesses us. He should have steered us this way. If He had done it another way, we would be where we wanted much quicker. This is much like having a toddler micromanage a parent's Christmas shopping. No parents I know take their children with them when shopping for their Christmas gifts . . . for good reason. When my son was a toddler, he was immediately drawn to any new toy he saw. He proclaimed loudly how much he wanted it and didn't even want to look around. As a parent, however, I had the perspective, experience in life, and reasoning abilities to decide which toys he would, in fact, enjoy the most instead of letting him settle for the first thing he saw. I would have never shopped for my son with the mental framework of "he would really enjoy that...so I'm going to get him something else he would enjoy less." If I, an earthly parent, do this, how much *more*, then, is God like that? God also, unlike us as humans, is unlimited in resources. Opening doors or supplying resources is never impossible or difficult for Him. He never says "no" due to budget. His decisions are always in line with His bigger plans—navigating His kids through the spiritual battles and victories of this life. Because of this, we can be certain that whatever He is giving us or whatever He is doing in our lives is truly the path of greatest fulfillment. He is a *good* father.

Thinking we have a better solution or greater insight than God, we are assuming we can out-create the creator. Any solution we have found or could think of is something God already knows. If the way He goes about fulfilling His promises in your life isn't the way you anticipate, I assure you it is because God has already thought of that solution and found it to be lacking for you in some way. We are creative and problem solvers *because* God created us in His image and we inherited some of His creative tendencies. But let me assure you, God is *the* Creator. For every amazing dream, good idea, redemptive story, or blessed outcome you could imagine, He imagines *bigger*.

"Every good and perfect gift is from above, coming down from the Father of the heavenly lights, who does not change like shifting shadows." James 1:17

TAKE IT TO GOD:

Ask each of these questions one at a time, and wait in the still silence for God's answer. Jot it down!

Highlight ways that my hope deferred has jaded me. Please send your love and comfort to heal those places now.

What are desires You have placed within me? What is your original intention for those desires? How have they gotten sidetracked or misused and ended up in disappointment?

*I'm taking you out of the box and letting You do it Your way,
God. Show me a situation that you're still working in that maybe I
have given up hope for or become bitter in.*

Chapter Five

DEFENSE AND OFFENSE

"I will defend this city and save it, for my sake and for the sake of David my servant!."

ISAIAH 37:35

DEFENSELESS

IF THERE'S ONE THING we don't want to be, it's defenseless. Sitting through one modern-day commercial break will tell you that. There are products to protect your heath, products to protect your money, products to protect your children, products to protect your confidential information. The world teaches that if you play good enough defense, you *might* be able to avoid some unpleasant situations. Risk mitigation sells. While I'm not calling preparedness a bad thing, many of the ways we attempt to defend ourselves are no better than a placebo. There is no amount of money that can purchase or good behavior that can earn a worry-free life. We juggle wielding our favorite cumbersome defense tactics—and, let's be honest, we all have our favorite DIY defense structures—without realizing that these shields are walling us in from our one true defense: God's love.

We defend ourselves from dark fears by numbing them with a TV binge. We defend ourselves from the pain of rejection of others by keeping our distance. We defend ourselves from failure by making sure we don't aim too high. We pacify our fears of death by plunging into diet fads and exercise regimens. We remedy our fear that God doesn't like us by cramming our days with ministry. What any one of these things does is just push away the cure. By our own merits, we are all defenseless.

Interestingly enough, Merriam Webster has two definitions for "defend". The first is "to drive danger or attack away from." The second is "to continue to declare to be true or proper despite opposition or objections." God is *always* our Defender. Sometimes it looks like driving away attack or danger. Other times it looks like *amidst* opposition and objections continuing to declare to you the *truth* beyond the attacks. In either case, the attack (there's no need for defense without an accuser) is *always* to shake our confidence in God's *love* for us. If the enemy can get us to feel unloved, he can shake our foundation of *trust* in God as well as leave the door propped wide open for *fear* to step in (since it's perfect love that drives out fear).

We see this also in people who have walls or defenses up against us. Whether that takes the form of being judgmental, being hesitant to let us in, or a variety of other forms, it usually has way more to do with them needing to receive love in a specific way than it ever did with you. Have compassion. Pray for them. Then, in turn, examine the ways that your defenses are triggered. If you feel that need to self-defend, self-promote, avenge, or self-explain, stop and take a minute to ask Holy Spirit to show you why your defenses feel weak in that area. Ask the Great Defender to cover that place in love. As you heal from the inside out, so will manifestations of those places in which we've adopted a defenseless spirit. We hear the term "orphan spirit." Orphans were literally defenseless. An orphan spirit says, "No one is going to defend me, so I have to look out for myself." Any area of you that is saying this, is in need of a major dose of love from the Father. Let His love wash over you and remove all of your defenses. Only then will you truly have the safety you long for. Only then can you make the Lord your refuge.

STRONGHOLDS

"Strongholds" has become a Biblical buzz word for places the enemy has kept control of in your life. A whole new meaning to this word found me one sunny day in the elementary school pick-up line waiting to get my son. I was looking up instances of this word in *Strong's Concordance* [1]when I found something game-changing. Strongholds were places of *perceived safety.* Like an old military defense, a stronghold is a fortress to which you retreat when everything is shaking. We can make the Lord our stronghold and defense, or we can make a false argument or idol a stronghold or defense. It shows which we've chosen when we are squeezed. While strongholds (good or bad) are a defense mechanism, we can tell what our strongholds are most easily by our plan of attack. What do we turn to to save us when we feel threatened? Words from people? Financial security? A health protocol? Or a cancelled day of plans to sit and worship? These responses don't "earn" a change in circumstances, but they wildly change how we navigate them, what we learn from them, and—many times—how long we stay stuck in them.

PLEASING SACRIFICES

Not having to "earn" our forgiveness or deliverance sounds amazing. The "gospel," or good news, is aptly named because it is, in fact, good news. Having our heart understood is such a relief. Thinking of the children's movie *The Incredibles*, I am reminded of Syndrome. He's the villain. The movie makes viewers privy to his backstory, which is one of wanting desperately to be a super hero and help while only being met by rejection. Seeing him function as an adult, you *know* this man's actions are wrong. There is no

1. Strong, *Strong's Expanded Exhaustive Concordance of the Bible,* 1655.

debate about his deviance. The more you understand his motivations and his character, however, the more you begin to feel mercy for this character. *This is not at all the same as approval of what he does*, but more of an understanding of the heart that's broken but good at the core that is motivating his actions. That does not change the morality of his actions, but you no longer hate him for them. You just long to see him get healed.

I feel like this is not far off from how God operates. He sees all we do right and all we miss the mark on. He doesn't, however, view it with condemnation. He views us with *mercy* because after Jesus's sacrifice we became His children and His friends. He *does* correct us and try to keep us from wrong, particularly when it is done deliberately, but He will never stop loving us, and He understands our motivations in a unique way. He just wants to see our needs met...in a way that is not spiritually or physically destructive to ourselves or others. The motivation behind every action, every redemption, every correction is always *love*.

Grace, our biggest comfort, also becomes our biggest challenge. Matthew 10:8 presents the challenge; "Freely you have received; freely give." Why is it so much more difficult to extend that kind of grace to others? Simply, our point of view renders us non-objective. We only know our piece of the puzzle. Our emotions, our consequences, our treatment. While we may know bits and pieces of the other side (and they may truly seem to deserve punishment), ultimately, we are not omniscient and cannot view all the moving pieces like our one Judge can. Our Judge, however, is also our Lawyer. He played our Advocate as Jesus became our guilt and was punished in our place. Now He stands at the right hand of the Father interceding for us! He is our Defense. You have a God that isn't looking for ways to find you guilty. He has plead your innocence through the blood of His Son!

SOLD OUT

Most of us don't have to think very far back to recall the last time we were offended or the last time someone really hurt our hearts.

Maybe you were treated unfairly. Maybe you were betrayed. Maybe you were let down. Humans are created to be very empathetic beings. It is one of our greatest gifts, but it can also be one of our biggest hurdles. From a young age we learn the golden rule and are quickly dissuaded from bad behavior when we realize what it's like to be on the receiving end of those actions. When someone hurts us, we (knowingly or unknowingly) assume that they don't understand our pain. This may or may not be true. We instinctively want those who hurt us to understand and feel the pain we are feeling. This births bitterness, unforgiveness, and the urge for revenge. Again, this urge to right wrongs comes from a good place. It comes from the piece of us that is made in our Father's image, and He is the great righter of wrongs. The problem is we are not God. Just as a young child doesn't know enough about his father's work to be able to fill in even just one day on the job for him, we don't know enough to fill in for God. Why, then, is it so hard to let it go?

Typically, unforgiveness is hard to let go of when we feel like it won't be dealt with. Sometimes there is this delusion from the enemy that if we don't take care of it that it will be ignored forever. That if we don't stand up for ourselves that no one will. But if we slow our emotions for a moment and think about it, would the God who went all the way to the cross for us not stand up for us? In fact, He already has.

Let's think of forgiveness as something that can be bought—because, in ways, it was purchased with Jesus's blood. It's as if God went to the store and purchased all the forgiveness that was ever made—enough for everyone to have it as many times as they needed it. Forgiveness is sold out. When something is sold out more cannot be purchased. It does not matter how much you want to pay for it, there simply is no more to be bought. It is already purchased.

God, however, didn't just buy all the forgiveness and hold on to it. He took this precious, precious thing called forgiveness and gave it to all of us. Obviously, that's the collective story of the Bible. The story of God's great forgiveness and love. Forgiveness has the power to completely restore and recreate in relationships. Instead of dooming the relationship to end in division, forgiveness offers a multitude of possibilities with endless ripple effects that spread out to the edges of eternity! This powerful, powerful thing was given to *us*. We see how with our own forgiveness it has allowed us to receive fresh starts and new paths many times over in each of our lives. But God didn't just give us forgiveness for us. He gave us the forgiveness meant for others too. *"If you forgive anyone's sins, their sins are forgiven; if you do not forgive them, they are not forgiven."* (John 20:23). Whoa. That is a heavy statement.

Alright, let's go back to the analogy of forgiveness being something you buy at the store. Withholding forgiveness is almost like having that person come to pick up their forgiveness (that is paid for by God) and then charging them when they get there. If you gave someone a gift card to his or her favorite store for Christmas, and you later found out that when they went to the store and redeemed their gift card that the store charged them anyway, you would be upset! You would be upset that your friend didn't get his or her gift, and you would be upset that the good money you paid for that gift card was essentially no good.

When others come to us for forgiveness (or, more often, when they don't even ask for forgiveness) and we refuse to forgive them, it's as if we are saying, "I know God paid for this in His blood, but I'm going to need *you* to pay as well." No wonder God seems upset at the idea of us not forgiving as we have been forgiven! It's like saying the high price He paid is no good.

Forgiving doesn't mean that the feelings will automatically go away. You may not *feel* like forgiving them, and that's ok. What's important is that you declare their forgiveness and pray for their blessing. Over time your soul will begin to align with your spirit and that emotional sting will be lessened. More importantly, you'll be right with the One who has paid for *your* forgiveness and who promises that He alone will avenge because He alone can do it perfectly.

FORGIVING *EVERYONE* INCLUDES YOU

Maybe you have done some extensive work in forgiveness. Maybe forgiveness comes more naturally to you as a spiritual gift. Praise God! When you ask yourself if there's anyone you need to forgive, there may truthfully not be anyone you can think of. Often times, though, we skip over a very important person: ourselves. Going back to the second greatest commandment ("And the second is like it: 'Love your neighbor as yourself.'" Matthew 22:39), many put the emphasis more on the "love your neighbor" part than the "as yourself" part when really the two should be equally emphasized. Using "as" implies a comparison that is *equal*. Certainly, God was pretty big on loving others, so we can assume from that verse that He is just as serious about us loving ourselves.

Not allowing ourself forgiveness is like going on a movie date with God and wearing a sleep mask. God has paid our ticket, yet we are refusing ourselves what He has paid for. The enemy may try to trick you into feeling like it is "noble" to let ourselves suffer for what we have done, but actually it's insulting to God. He paid for our forgiveness (or our ticket, using my analogy), and for us to refuse to enjoy it is disappointing.

God has a long line of flawed forefathers to remind us that we are no exception. Moses is one of my personal favorites. Here's why. Remember how Moses is always putting himself down about not being a good speaker? Well, the Holy Spirit, when speaking through Steven in Acts chapter seven as he addresses the Sanhedrin, totally blows his cover. In verse 22, Stephen says of Moses, "Moses was educated in all the wisdom of the Egyptians and was powerful in speech and action." *Powerful* in speech and action. What sent him on a self-deprecating spiral that led to him barely agreeing to deliver the people of Israel? My guess is a little bout of unforgiveness for himself. Continuing in Stephen's speech it says:

> *"When Moses was forty years old, he decided to visit his own people, the Israelites. He saw one of them being mistreated by an Egyptian, so he went to his defense and avenged him by killing the Egyptian. Moses thought that*

his own people would realize that God was using him to rescue them, but they did not. The next day Moses came upon two Israelites who were fighting. He tried to reconcile them by saying, 'Men, you are brothers; why do you want to hurt each other?'"But the man who was mistreating the other pushed Moses aside and said, 'Who made you ruler and judge over us? Are you thinking of killing me as you killed the Egyptian yesterday?' When Moses heard this, he fled to Midian, where he settled as a foreigner and had two sons."

Acts 7:23–29

The first time I truly read that my heart leapt with compassion and empathy. Moses *thought that his own people would realize God was using him to rescue them.* This makes me think Moses had to have had a Word from the Lord that he *knew* was over his life. He *knew* God was going to use him to rescue the Israelites. Moses acted in *offense* when he thought he to *defend* his calling (rather than leaving it to God), and he wound up acting outside of the will of God. His *intent* was peace. His *intent* was fulfilling God's call on his life. When a word of *attack* was launched at him the next day, it didn't take a single person driving Moses out of His promised land. He exiled himself. For forty years he was in self-imposed exile before the Lord had to resurrect his calling and confidence. Ironically, the same forty-year struggle those he would lead would face in the desert.

Fast forward, when Moses is penning all these laws for God (because ironically God was still using this guy who thinks he's not good at words to write down all His words), he says an interesting thing. He writes, (in Exodus 21:12–13) "*Anyone who strikes a person with a fatal blow is to be put to death. However, if it is not done intentionally, but God lets it happen, they are to flee to a place I will designate.*" I can't help but hear Moses's own voice, still struggling to reconcile his own failures and God's laws . . . "if it's not intentional . . . .but God lets it happen . . . ." Was he still trying to forgive himself? We don't know. We do know God does not like murder. We also know God loves Moses. He loves Aaron the idolater. He loves David the adulterer. He loves Peter the liar. He loves you. He loves me. Let's love us too. Let's receive His forgiveness and "go and sin no more," as Jesus said to the woman caught in adultery. Let's not let a careless attack from the enemy send us into a self-imposed exile. More importantly, let's not let unforgiveness of ourselves teach those following us to wander or quit early. If you need to extend forgiveness to yourself, do it today. Don't wait. Enjoy what God has paid for and use that precious second chance to make it worth it.

DISCIPLINE NOT DISAPPROVE

While we are to completely release ourselves so that we are free from the chains of our own unforgiveness, we are also to keep from indulging ourselves. There is a difference—and you don't need to be a Biblical scholar to recognize it—between extending grace to ourselves and turning a blind eye to sin in the name of "not being perfect." We are accepting God's redirection and correction by owning when we have been wrong. On the flip side, God does discipline us, but many mistake His discipline for disapproval. This is also missing the mark.

I *love* the word *"discipline"*. Now before you put this book down and decide that you and I no longer have anything in common, let me explain. Discipline comes from the word "disciple." Disciples were those Jesus taught. He didn't teach them by berating them or beating them into the ground. He taught through example, loving relationship, and training them in a new direction of thinking. Similarly, "disciplines" are to be taught and learned.

The most vivid image that comes to my mind is a young student learning the martial arts. The instructor disciplines the student. If it is truly a good teacher, this doesn't mean the teacher yells at the kid, tells them they are bad, dislikes them, or punishes them. Read that again. God is not yelling at you. God is not telling you that you are bad. God *likes* you. God is *not* punishing you. He does not disapprove of you. Instead, discipline looks like the coach saying "try changing your grip," "aim a little to the left," or "don't forget to breathe." While these are corrections, the heart behind them is not accusatory. We have an accuser, and it is *not* God. Revelation 12:10 refers to the *enemy* as "accuser of our brothers and sisters." God's heart is our *helper*. John 14:26 says "The *Helper*, the Holy Spirit, whom the Father will send in my name, will teach you everything and make you remember all that I have told you." His discipline should not make us feel like garbage. Instead, His discipline should be received as "Oh! So that's how you do that better. Thanks for the help!"

"OF-*FENCES*"

Fences, as beautiful as they can appear, always divide. The question is, are you dividing yourself from the right things? The word instructs us to guard our hearts. What do we guard against, and are we erecting the correct types of dividers? Boundaries are wonderful-even essential! But we must establish them in the right places.

How would you feel about your neighbors putting up an eight-foot-tall barbed wire fence between their property and yours? How would you feel about a lion enclosure at the zoo being fenced in by a small picket fence? While both seem a silly or even offensive choice, many of us suffer from doing one or both of these very things in our spiritual lives.

We were built for community. As we put together pieces of Scripture, a look at our collective identity emerges. We were made in God's image (Gen. 1:27). God is love (1 John 4:8). *We* are, therefore, *made* to be *love*. God (who has no need of anything because... well... He's God) is Himself a trinity. He exists *in relationship*. That relationship is ever-expanding as His creation continues. More and more and more are invited into His love each day. Should that not be the case for us? When it comes to our neighbors sometimes our fences are too high. We have a comfortable circle of people we know and sometimes don't look for opportunity to expand it. We don't speak to those we don't know at the grocery store because we don't want to know them. We don't feel love for strangers because it's beyond our capacity to love *everyone*...isn't it? That would be true if we loved with *our* love.

We love because He first loved us. 1 John 4:19

God's love is the gas in our heart's gas tank. It runs out pretty quickly unless we refill. I have those words from 1 John 4:19 etched on a sign that sits on my kitchen counter. Days where I feel pretty wrung dry, I remember the truth. My supply is not limited to my supply. Each time we take time to let ourselves soak up God's love in its various forms (through His words to us, His miracles in our lives, the people He places in our lives, etc.), we refill ourselves to give out more love. The best way to feel love when you feel lonely? Give it away. Pray for God to show you someone to send a loving word to. Don't ask for this with the motivation of getting a certain response from that person, but do it simply out of a desire to bless and love him or her. Then watch how as you deliver love you feel God depositing love within you. It's not only love to give out but love to fill your own heart too! Instead of loving when we want to be loved, our instinct is most often to retreat behind our sky-high barbed wire fences and wait until someone finally scales them to love us. This is a lot like being dehydrated and deciding to sit down and wait until it rains. People's affections, like the rain, are largely out of our control. What we can do is get up, and go to the river of God's love to drink deeply. Chances are, we will also meet lots of other thirsty souls who came to drink as well.

Sounds beautiful, right? Some of you may be thinking, "As poetic as that sounds, what does going to the river even look like?" Some of you may interpret that as drinking solely from God's love and shunning nourishment from human affections. God wants us to nurture each other! He does not, however, want us to go to others with our thirst. He wants us to go to Him in prayer. Ask Him specifically for ways you can be a messenger of His love for someone else that day. I have found that as backward as that sounds (and many renewed mind principles do sound backwards), when you are actively praying for and contributing to the needs of others, yours somehow have a miraculous way of being met. God's love has a way of chasing you down and surprising you with the very blessings you ached for in the first place.

PICKET FENCES

Boundaries are essential. That's why we have our picket fences. They are not a deterrent for others to not draw near to us but rather a reminder that the space is *ours* to freely invite others in and out as we are given the discernment to do so. That superpower of choice comes back into play again. God honors our choices about those with whom we invest our time. He may not agree with them (and seeking His advice is strongly recommended), but He allows us to choose.

The body was such a good choice as an analogy for the church. The boundaries between the finger and fingernail are much different than the boundaries between hip and toe. Some people you just need more space between. Our command is to love, and we have to find the best proximity from which to do so. While we are created to love everyone, we are not created with the capacity to be everyone's best friend. Enjoy the close relationships. Enjoy the more distant ones. Each type of relationship supplies a vital two-way exchange of important truths both about yourself and the world. God uses it *all* for good. The best way to approach a relationship is to ask God, "what are you showing me in this relationship about how you created me?" ,"what pieces of Your heart and character can you use me to display for them?", "what pieces of Your heart and character can you use them to show me?", and "how can I learn and grow from in this relationship?"

Keep in mind that distance and bitterness are cousins. If your distance from someone stems from a feeling of bitterness or unforgiveness, then that unforgiveness can actually be harmful to you. Take the steps to forgive them and verbally release them in prayer from any judgments, anger, jealousy, or anything else that has been held against them. Then take the extra step that really kicks bitterness in the teeth. Pray for them to be *blessed*. While the distance may stay the same, those feelings will eventually turn to those of peace.

The quickest way to peace for me has been in that moment of bitterness—that moment of what feels like self-righteous rage. When it's so tempting to let that delicious hurt sink in, it changes everything to remember what Jesus did. He took beatings. He took abuse. He took slander. He took betrayal. He took fair-weather friendship. He took lies. He took disbelief. He took rage and abuse. Never once, however, did he take the battle into His own hands. He turned it over the God whose capable hands can handle defending Him, and He kept doing His job (which is now our job). He loved.

BARBED WIRE

We have established that we have an enemy. The enemy is *not* each other. Those barbed wire fences around our hearts need to be set up against what Scripture advises we guard against. The closest scriptural approximation to putting up barbed wire is the Ephesians 6 instructions to put on our spiritual armor. I love the Holy Spirit through Paul opens with a very fatherly reminder to be obedient. Just like I bend down to eye-level with my little boy and tell him, "I want you to listen to me and daddy," I picture God bending down in a posture—not of belittling—but of tender pleading in order that we can have the safest spiritual experience. What follows is *how* to be obedient in guarding our hearts.

> *Put on the full armor of God, so that you can take your stand against the devil's schemes. For our struggle is not against flesh and blood, but against the rulers, against the authorities, against the powers of this dark world and against the spiritual forces of evil in the heavenly realms. Therefore, put on the full armor of God, so that when the day of evil comes, you may be able to stand your ground, and after you have done everything, to stand. Stand firm then, with the belt of truth buckled around your waist, with the breastplate of righteousness in place, and with your feet fitted with the readiness that comes from the gospel of peace. In addition to all this, take up the shield of*

*faith, with which you can extinguish all the flaming arrows
of the evil one. Take the helmet of salvation and the sword
of the Spirit, which is the word of God.*

Ephesians 6:11–17

Right at the outset we are told exactly what should be on the
other side of the barbed wire around our hearts; the enemy, dark
powers in the world, and forces of evil in the heavenlies. It's interesting to note that these are listed separately. There are forces
working against God's purposes here in the natural world, and
there are also forces of evil working against God's purposes in the
supernatural. Both are to be guarded against, but neither are to be
feared. God instructs time and time again, *not* to fear. In fact, the
only times the Bible tells us to fear someone it is God Himself. This
kind of fear is not a cowering terror but more a deeply respect-
ful longing to please because we acknowledge just how vital and
powerful God is.

To guard against both natural and supernatural powers of
evil there are not two protocols given but one. The armor, this
barbed wire of protection that alerts us as to *when* we should have
our guard up and *how* to effectively keep the good in and the bad
out, is actually a protocol. Let's look at each piece one by one. Each
piece of armor clues us in to what we are guarding against. By
looking at the weapon we are given, we can deduce the attack it
protects against.

The belt of truth is first. If our *defense* is truth, we can assume
the enemy's offense is *lies*. Scripture confirms this suspicion, telling
us in many occasions to guard against false teaching (Ezekiel 13:9,
Jeremiah 23:16, Matthew 24:24, Matthew 16:11–12, 2 Timothy
4:3–4, Acts 20:30, 1 John 4:1, Matthew 7:15, and many more!). We
can test what we take in by making sure it isn't distorting what we
already know God says in scripture and, in the case of prophecy,
seeing if it comes to pass.

> *You may say to yourselves, "How can we know when a mes-
> sage has not been spoken by the Lord?" If what a prophet
> proclaims in the name of the Lord does not take place or*

come true, that is a message the Lord has not spoken. That
prophet has spoken presumptuously, so do not be alarmed.

Deuteronomy 18:21–22

The next piece of armor is our breastplate of righteousness. We wouldn't need a breastplate of righteousness if there was not an attack coming against us to make us believe we are unrighteous. The entire message of the gospel is that *because of the sacrifice of Jesus, we are made righteous by having faith that He has saved us.* Any message communicating that we must earn our redemption or are too far for grace to cover is dangerous and must be kept well on the other side of our barbed wire fence. Why? Because being saved by grace through faith because of Jesus's sacrifice is the thesis of God's story for us. Without it we have missed the point entirely.

"Readiness of the gospel of peace" is one of those phrases that even those with tattered, well-read Bible pages have to stop and look at one piece at a time. Readiness. It's a state that is best equated with camping soldiers or expectant parents. It's that feeling of being ready to go whenever the time may come. Soldiers who are camped in waiting, ready for when the signal is given to launch the attack. Parents who have spent nine months preparing for this unborn child and have a bag packed and waiting by the door for a time only God knows. Readiness.

It's a stark contrast with the word peace. Peace brings to mind totally release and relaxation. But the thing that knits the two together in perfectly sensical way—the bridge from constant readiness and perpetual peace—is that beautiful word "gospel." Our gospel, our "good news", is not only that Jesus's sacrifice was real, personal, and final, but it's all the repercussions of that sacrifice. Death has been forever taken away. It is traded for eternal life. Our problems in this world are no longer only our own, but our constant companion is the God who is mightier than anything we could come up against. Our power is also not our own, but we have become shells drained of our mortal power and old selves and refilled with the selves we were designed to be. We are equipped as conduits of the Father's power to do all Jesus did *and even greater things.* Now *that*, my friends, is the good news. And that kind of news brings both readiness—being ready to go anywhere, do anything, at any time, for anyone, regardless of the impossibilities involved—*as well as* peace—that we go not by our own power but with supernatural force working in us and through us and a mandate that's not our own but one ensured by the heavenlies.

So, what clues does this give us to attacks we are to guard against? If we are not equipped with readiness, we are stuck. We are overly cautious. We are discouraged. We are more overcome by the things against us than the things motivating us. If we are not equipped with peace, we are flooded with fear, gripped by worry, and rocked by uncertainty. In essence, we become either erratic or dormant. These things need to be carefully locked out of our hearts. If, from time to time, they sneak back in, kick them out! They belong on the other side of that barbed wire.

We are also given a shield of faith. Faith is having *trust* that is not based on what we see but is instead based on our beliefs. The opposite of faith is distrust or doubt. This threatens to sneak into our hearts and poison the well. This is exactly why the Word urges us to guard our hearts above all else because all things flow from the heart. The remedy for attacks of doubt or mistrust is to remember our *faith*. The best way to do this is, firstly, feeding on testimonies. Nothing peps up the spirit more than remembering what used to feel impossible and then happened by God's grace. Recall what used to be your fervent prayer request and now is your reality. Then, remind yourself of His pending promises. He's been faithful. He will be faithful. And He's not finished.

Our shield's faithful companion is the sword of the Spirit which our armor passage in Ephesians tells us is the word of God. In order to have faith, we have to know first what we believe and what to have faith in. This isn't left to supposition. God gives us His word so we know *exactly* the stance to take. Everything He promises stays safely inside our hearts, while all that tempts us to disbelieve those promises remains outside our fence. The attack that we need the sword of the Spirit against is actually usually the twisting, distortion, or misperception of God's words and promises. That's why we are given a tool that it says divides even down to *intention*. It allows to not just accept was sounds good but what truly *is* good.

Finally, we get to that wonderful head of yours—that amazing hunk of cells with the astounding ability to contemplate all of this. Our heads are protected spiritually by *salvation*. I think there is something significant to God making this the spiritual protection for our heads. Back in Biblical days it was a huge sign of victory to display the head of your enemy. It meant power and prowess. Our head—our mind—is exactly what the enemy wants most. He would love to slip into our thoughts and steer our thinking to derail us from God's plans for us.

After our daughter was born, I got a medical test result back, and it was the kind you don't want to get. On the way home, through a mouthful of French fries, I blubbered to my husband that this was it. I had gone full DEFCON 1 on this test result and decided I was about to have a long health battle in front of me—if I even survived at all! I prayed. I repented. I wept. I reminisced. I told a few close friends and had them praying. They decided to repeat the test in a few months. Same result. My heart sank. They now had to move to more extensive testing. The biopsy was scheduled. I waited for a call for the results and remained in my self-imposed dying hole, biding my time. When the call came . . . everything was normal. They had found nothing even down to a cellular level. I wasn't "healed". They just had finally gotten conclusive enough testing to find out I was never sick. These six months of waiting taught me something, though. It taught me that the battle is in our mind. My body was never even an issue, yet I was in the trenches like someone fighting cancer. I had to overcome the battle in my mind *regardless* of what was going on with my body if I was ever going to get victory. I had to come to the conclusion that I couldn't "earn" my health. I couldn't "do the right things" and guarantee my future. Each day, simply put, is just a gift from God. I know very Godly people who struggle with sickness and people who couldn't care less about the Lord who are in perfect health. I may never fully understand the "why's," but I understand that I cannot save myself. But the beautiful release in that is that God isn't waiting on or expecting me to save myself either.

If the defense given to us against attacks like those is *salvation,* there is something profound locked in that picture. "Salvation" is defined by Merriam-Webster to mean "deliverance from the power and effects of sin," "liberation from ignorance or illusion," or "preservation from destruction or failure." Hear this. The enemy wants you to feel trapped in your sin *or* in the *effects* of your sin. He wants you to be ignorant of your power. He wants to give the illusion that your calling is all a lie and you have no hope. He wants you to feel like a failure that is headed toward imminent destruction. Friends, have you *felt* these attacks before? I know I have. Let's put on our helmet as we *put these truths into our minds.* You are *totally* delivered. You are *free* from ignorance and have been given the mind of Christ to comprehend the mysteries of heaven which God reveals to you. You are *free* from illusions of the world that come against the word of God. You have been totally and *eternally* preserved and protected by God Himself from destruction or failure. All you have to do is just accept it. Take it, put it on, and put that fence up.

Adopt a zero-tolerance policy for anything that resembles what God tells us to guard against. The enemy cannot overtake you, but he can tempt you to surrender the whole fortress. He knows he cannot overcome your Defense (the Lord), so he tempts you to take refuge or make your strongholds in places that are not God. The renewed mind is one that stands side-by-side with God, hands over the blueprints of the property of his or her life, and carries out His suggestions as He shows you how to tear down fences that should never have been there and build others that have been gravely needed.

> Above all else, guard your heart, for everything you do flows from it.
>
> Proverbs 4:23

TAKE IT TO GOD:

Ask each of these questions one at a time, and wait in the still silence for God's answer. Jot it down!

How do I have my defenses built up against You? OR how have I tried to become my own defender instead of letting You defend me?

Open my eyes to a deeper level of how You are my Defender. Remind me of testimonies of Your defense.

In what ways do I need to forgive/love others?

In what ways do I need to forgive/love myself?

God how are you disciplining (DISCIPLE-ING) me right now and what skill is that growing in me?

Where have I placed picket fences where barbed wire must be placed?

Where have I placed barbed wire where a picket fence should be?

Chapter Six

Your Mission
(Should You Choose to Accept It)

"Then Jesus came to them and said, 'All authority in heaven and on earth has been given to me. Therefore, go and make disciples of all nations, baptizing them in the name of the Father and of the Son and of the Holy Spirit, and teaching them to obey everything I have commanded you. And surely, I am with you always, to the very end of the age'."

Matthew 28:18–20

"I will make you into a great nation, and I will bless you; I will make your name great, and you will be a blessing. I will bless those who bless you, and whoever curses you I will curse, and all peoples on earth will be blessed through you."

Genesis 12:2–3

ONE GOAL, DIFFERENT ROLES

Whiz. An arrow flies and, with perfect precision, frightens the horse who topples his rider. *Whiz.* A second arrow, expertly launched, pins the enemy to the ground. This kind of silver screen battle scene is familiar to most of us. In chapter one we compared arrows to purposes. God has equipped you with quiver full of arrows. These little purposes for which we were created may all be different from each other and from anyone else's purposes, but they are all fighting the *same battle* regardless of whether we realize it or not. This is why Jesus said, "Whoever is not with me is against me, and whoever does not gather with me scatters." (Matthew 12:30). In our battle scene analogy, each arrow does a different task in battle, but the collective task of them all is to defeat the efforts of the enemy and *take more ground*. We are all created to take more ground for the Kingdom of God. Unfortunately, many are under the impression that the battle is over and all ground has been won. With the invention of the internet, surely everyone is evangelized by now, right? Wrong.

Jesus charged us with our great commission in Matthew chapter 28 to make disciples of all nations—all peoples. This is not a new commissioning but a reiteration of what we were purposed for all the way back in Genesis when God told Abraham every people group on earth would be blessed through him. Thus far we haven't achieved it. Many are shocked to know that according to current *Joshua Project* statistics more than three billion people on the planet are still considered unreached. "Unreached" for these statistics means that the evangelical Christian population in that area is less than two percent. This number doesn't even include potentially billions more that have heard of Jesus but never encountered Him. *The Christian Post* found, however, that on average Americans spend more money on Halloween costumes for dogs than funding Christ-centered efforts in these unreached areas. As spiritual children of Abraham, the promise that *all* people on the earth will be blessed through him is ours. That's a promise that has been spoken by God, and not a single of His words returns void. If there are still people in the world who have not had their lives radically blessed by the transforming and restorative power of Jesus then we're simply not done.

NOT YOUR OWN

A certain renewing of the mind occurs when everything is viewed through the lens of this specific purpose. It changes how you see the person on the street corner holding a sign. It changes the conversation you have in the line at the supermarket. It changes your vacations into mission trips. Your children become the next generation in training. Your resources become opportunities to be a blessing. Everything takes on different priority and greater meaning through the lens of our collective and individual purposes. There are billions of people to reach. And God looked at that task and said, "Ok, we need a *you.*"

> *Do you not know that your bodies are temples of the Holy Spirit, who is in you, whom you have received from God? You are not your own; you were bought at a price. Therefore, honor God with your bodies.*

1 Corinthians 6:19–20

Our actions, our resources, our relationships, our careers, our families -our everything—is by design and are tools in this ultimate mission. Everything you have and everything you do can be wielded like a spiritual weapon to make an impact in this larger fight. We can't finish the mission Jesus started, however, if we still don't acknowledge that the Great Commission applies to us.

GO AND MAKE DISCIPLES

Making disciples doesn't look like placing a bulk order of Biblical-style robes and finding a tribe willing to follow you. It also doesn't mean you have to have all your imperfections and kinks worked out to be qualified to lead. If that were the case, we'd all be waiting forever to be worthy to lead. It is the cycle of becoming like a spiritual trail guide. There are parts of the trail of walking in faith that you have trudged through with a level of familiarity and learning such that you can recognize every twig and leaf. Jesus has shown you how to navigate the terrain, and you now have some valuable leadership skills for that particular trail. For every trail you've been down with the Lord, however, there's still many, many more you haven't. There's always more to learn if you're still this side of Heaven, and that's the fun part.

One thing I *always* tell our teenagers (my husband and I have been youth pastors for several years now) is to pray and seek God each season on who you can be discipling and who you can be discipled by. It doesn't matter if you're a middle-schooler—there is an elementary-aged believer who would love to learn what you're learning from Jesus. While age usually has a lot to do with how much we've gotten to gain from the Lord, it isn't *always* an indicator of discipleship. Sometimes God brings a peer alongside you who has simply walked the road you're on before you. The beauty in discipleship is the ripples.

Look at a map of Canada. Canada's terrain is riddled with lakes. If you wanted to make a wave across the country, throwing one stone wouldn't work. If you were to throw a stone in one lake, you'd surely make some ripples. They may even carry all the way to shore. The ripples would never, however, jump land and affect another lake. Unless you threw another rock. Each of us is strategically placed. We have influence on a "lake" or two, spiritually speaking. If Jesus drops a great nugget of wisdom into my life, I can share it with my youth group or my blog. These "lakes" would then also get to benefit from that teaching of the Lord. It wouldn't go far beyond that though. Unless some of those who were *discipled* by that teaching then taught it to their own *disciples* outside of those groups. Now we're pond-jumping. You jump a few ponds, and you're across the world. Literally. So, if you don't feel like the wisest or most qualified to lead, great! That's a good sign of humility. Let me encourage you with the fact that it's not *your* leadership or *your* wisdom the world needs anyway. It's God's. The only reason I have anything to fill these pages with that may be remotely useful is the Holy Spirit's wisdom—both wisdom I've directly received in my own life walking with Him *and* the wisdom that I've received from those who have *discipled* me that have passed on their wisdom from Him as well. We're all in this together. And someone's journey starts with you going and making disciples.

WE HAVE IN ORDER TO GIVE

"What could I have to give?" you may be asking yourself. Being able to give begins with sharpening your focus on what you *have to give*. That's just it. You *have* in order to *give*. When I began writing this book, I actually got an image of an "uncommon vessel"—the ones made for special purposes—being broken on the bottom. A big hole appeared in the pottery, making it completely useless in the eyes of the world but *priceless* in the eyes of God. Things poured into the vessel would merely leak right out the bottom. The difference in what we call priceless and useless depends on what kind of mind we are thinking with. The mind of the world sees value in *holding* things and uselessness in giving it all. "The more you have, the more you're worth," says the world. "The more you *give*, the more you will be *given*" says the renewed mind. The renewed mind sees uselessness in holding things but great value in *being poured into in order to pour out to others*. The renewed mind realizes that daily-renewed resources didn't start or stop with manna. The *evidence* of this realization (the action that results from having this faith) is living like you have a God who gives daily provision.

> *What good is it, my brothers and sisters, if someone claims to have faith but has no deeds? Can such faith save them? Suppose a brother or sister is without clothes or daily food. If one of you says to them, "Go in peace; keep warm and well fed," but does nothing about their physical needs, what good is it? In the same way, faith by itself, if it is not accompanied by action, is dead.*
>
> James 2:14-17

IN THE BEGINNING

In the garden, before the fall, when things were perfect, God's "mission" to Adam and Eve was this:

> Then God said, "Let us make mankind in our image, in our likeness, so that they may rule over the fish in the sea and the birds in the sky, over the livestock and all the wild animals, and over all the creatures that move along the ground." So, God created mankind in his own image, in the image of God he created them male and female he created them. God blessed them and said to them, "Be fruitful and increase in number; fill the earth and subdue it. Rule over the fish in the sea and the birds in the sky and over every living creature that moves on the ground." Then God said, "I give you every seed-bearing plant on the face of the whole earth and every tree that has fruit with seed in it. They will be yours for food. And to all the beasts of the earth and all the birds in the sky and all the creatures that move along the ground—everything that has the breath of life in it—I give every green plant for food." And it was so. God saw all that he had made, and it was very good. And there was evening, and there was morning—the sixth day.
>
> *Genesis 1:26–31*

Adam and Eve's mission in verse 28 (and ours too!) is be fruitful and increase. That word for be fruitful in Hebrew is *parah*[1] which *Strong's Concordance* defines as "bring forth (fruit), be, cause to be, make fruitful, grow, and increase." This creative command requires *action* of tending to what God had created for the purpose of *increasing* what His harvest on the earth. The next instruction God gives them is to "fill the earth and subdue it." The vision was a world full of people who were workers for the Kingdom. The word "subdue" used in verse 28 is the Hebrew word *kabash*[2] which, defined by *Strong's* means "to bring into bondage or to make subservient." Going even deeper, that word "subservient" carries with the connotation of *an obedience that doesn't waver or*

1. Strong, *Strong's Expanded Exhaustive Concordance of the Bible*, 1560.
2. Strong, *Strong's Expanded Exhaustive Concordance of the Bible*, 1514.

question. Subservient, closely tied to "servant" reminds us of being less important than in order to serve a purpose. Before the fall, this was easy! All things were pliable clay in the hands of the Potter and were used for the service of the Kingdom of God. Adam and Eve were the administrators of the King, making sure what was happening with every plant and animal and seed was in line with God's command. So, from the beginning, the instructions—the mission—was to *use*, *tend*, and *multiply* everything for the glory of God and to literally fill the earth with people doing the same.

THE BIGGEST LIE OF STEWARDSHIP

With that incredible equipping, Adam and Eve began with a world full of things to steward and total clarity on the job to be done. Until one question was raised. This same question is the one that attacks our modern-day stewardship when God prompts us to write a $500 check for someone "because He said so." It's the same question we face when we're about to step out in an area of our gifting, when we go up for the dream promotion, or when we prepare to board the plane for that international assignment. There's that little question of "did God really say?" When it was first posed by the serpent in Genesis 3 verse 1, that "obedience that doesn't waver or question" wavered. Without renewing our mind, we waver today as well.

HOW TO MULTIPLY

The Word of God is filled with stories of those who made what they had (however small) subservient to God's purposes, and it *multiplied*. Even Jesus Himself teaches it in the parable of the talents. At the very beginning, the parable clearly says that the man entrusted *his* wealth to his servants. It belonged to him. They served him. This wasn't a loan from a buddy. There was no doubt about the expectation that there was *work to be done* with the money. The first servant, it says, went *at once* and put the money to work. No holding back. The same was true for the second servant. I actually love that while they were trusted with different amounts, *both had the same growth ratio*. Both reaped double for their master. I also love that the response from the master to both of these servants is word for word the same. I think that's no accident. It shows that there's no difference in how Jesus rewards or views the steward-ship of those who are entrusted with much versus those entrusted with less. The first servant technically had a larger sum to give back to the Master upon his return, but *that made no difference in the Master thinking the servant had done well, or the upgrade to more, or the invitation to share in the Master's joy.*

He didn't say "Oh, good job. But Frank did better." He also didn't say "You did good. I'm going to keep you doing exactly what you're doing because I know you can handle that, but I'm not sure you're ready for more." It also wasn't, "Hey thanks! This is a great win for me. I appreciate you just being a pawn and serving my purposes." Rather it was universal, unconditional *celebration* and *elevation*. Because the servants were partnering and prospering and multiplying what belonged to the Master in creative ways, there was a *two-fold joy* in which the cooperation of Master and servant was prospering *both* of them.

That third servant though. That's the part that you skim through thinking "yikes!... weeping and gnashing of teeth, no thanks!" The most recent time I read through this parable, how-ever, God showed me this in a way I have never seen it.

The third servant starts in a way the first two don't. I always read it as an excuse—and it is—but it's more than that. He says, "I knew that you were a hard man, harvesting where you have not sown and gathering where you have not scattered seed." *Ouch!* He has the complete wrong idea of the Master. By calling him hard, the meanings attached to it were harsh, severe, or even offensive. That doesn't sound like the guy that just responded to the first two servants.

Then this servant tells him, essentially, that what he has isn't even rightfully his—that he harvests where he hasn't sown and gathers where he hasn't scattered. This leads me to wonder . . . who did the servant think scattered the seed that yielded the harvest for this Master? Maybe servants like himself? If so, this bitter servant may have truly seen this as the Master getting some of what was rightfully his. We can't know for sure, but, if that's the case, he forgot who *bought* every single seed. He forgot who provided his living. Regardless of the "why," we know for sure that he buried what he was entrusted with because something in him *feared* (he literally says he was afraid) that any other outcome wouldn't be advantageous *for himself*. He had totally lost sight of the cooperative mindset of multiplication that comes with a Kingdom yoke.

Don't we all do that? Don't we sometimes get all sorts of wild ideas about what could personally happen to us if we put what God has given us on the line and take leaps of faith to make it grow? Do we accuse God of being harsh sometimes? Offensive? Severe? Are we ever even a *little* afraid that if we give Him our heart, our money, our career, our time, our talent, or whatever else that the outcome won't be advantageous for us? In those moments we forget that not only is God a God that is always inviting us into more and more and greater and greater, but we also forget that every single thing we do for Him is *an invitation to share in His happiness*. His happiness is our happiness. Wow.

In responding to this third servant, the Master never confirms his accusations of him. He never says, "Yeah you're right. I am like that." I almost hear the heartbreak in his voice as he echoes the accusation back, checking, "so this is what you think?" So as you read this I ask you to ponder . . . what do *you* think of your Master?

I notice another difference with the third servant. The first two servants are *active* in their approach to what they've been given. Some translations say they traded to increase their sums. Other translations say they "gained" more. Either way, we know it was something they actively did with what they were given. In the Master's reply to the third servant, He says (in my own interpretation) something to the effect of, "Man, you could've done *something—anything*! Even giving it to the bank—a trustworthy place in which it can accumulate interest. Just don't bury it!!"

Is it just a coincidence that we bury things that are dead? What else was dead in that third servant? His hope? His love? His confidence that he would be taken care of? What is dead in you that keeps you from investing? Let God bring it back to *life*!

Then the third servant gets thrown outside. In the dark. Weeping and gnashing of teeth. Sounds a lot like the fall. Thrown out of the Garden. Spiritually in the dark. All of a sudden there's pain and worry. Toil. Work was supposed to be a joy! In fact, work was supposed to be much more than that. That parable is so often seen strictly as a financial one, but I want to challenge you today to look at it today through a few new lenses. What have you been given?

TITLES, TITHE, TALENTS, TIME

"What do you do?" is one of the first questions we ask each other. It's hard to separate who we are from our titles. Even Jesus was known by His titles.

> *"Isn't this the carpenter? Isn't this Mary's son and the brother of James, Joseph, Judas and Simon? Aren't his sisters here with us?" And they took offense at him."*
>
> *Mark 6:3*

They were deeply offended and refused to believe in him. Carpenter. Son. Brother. I often wonder at what went on during Jesus' gap time that the gospels don't detail. He obviously spent many years as a carpenter, learning Joseph's trade and practicing it himself. Since His life reflected the perfect will of God, there's got to be value in him having a profession. Similarly, there's value in Him having a family. He could've just "poofed" down here, but he was a son. And not just that...a brother and a friend. A renewed mind isn't about separating you from what you do. It's challenging you to make what you do and our mission as believers *inseparable*.

On my journey to what would become co-founding One Spark International, God taught me so much about titles. I got to see professionals in almost any field you can imagine—teachers, business people, agricultural experts, and IT guys to name a few—use their talents to lead Christian businesses, and organizations in those unreached areas of the world. If they were an engineer, they worked as an engineer. They did their job well. They loved people. They authentically lived their lives. They were not living a cover or alias. They are being genuinely themselves. A genuinely amazing engineer. Who is genuinely in love with Jesus. And God took it from there. We'd see Muslims getting baptized, churches be born and *grow,* and movements of God ignite. These miracles were not led by our professionals either. The icing on the cake is that they were led by the people around them. Ordinary people who saw an ordinary engineer say he's going to pray about business decisions. Or families whose child had a teacher who was uncommonly generous. Factory workers who were astounded by their business owner that actually cares for his staff in a way that's not normal. Normal people who the locals came to know had a God who was anything but normal.

Titles

Ironically, the year God told me to quit my job and work for Him, the work He had for me was to help others use their work for Him. It's downright funny. Talk about multiplication! I never realized how much our work mattered to God until I learned one Hebrew word: *abodah*[3].

Essentially, in Hebrew, there is no word that means "ministry" the way we use it today. Our modern day use falls along the lines of "Oh, he's in ministry", or "They left their jobs to go into full time ministry." That "ministry" word is "*abodah.*" It means, according to *Strongs Concordance* something way closer to "work and service" as in work or service to the temple by the priests but also work and service in everyday life. They were the same word! Think about your titles; professional titles, family titles, volunteer work, etc. Now think—that is your *worship.* We are all ministers, and your

3. Strong, *Strong's Expanded Exhaustive Concordance of the Bible,* 1547.

work is your worship. What titles has God placed in our hands? How are we investing them to serve and multiply the Kingdom?

Tithe

Money is the most obvious application when we think of the parable of the talents. The tithe is a well-known concept. Many wonder why this Old Testament concept stuck around while others (such as the obtuse regulations for skin diseases in Leviticus 13) did not. You may have heard the argument, "if we're released from the law and are under grace, doesn't that include the tithe?" Yes and no. This is not a legalistic adherence to an Old Testament law in order to earn prosperity or salvation. Offering a tithe is a *starting place* for the New Testament's renewed mind generosity. The Old Testament gave the first fruits amount of ten percent. The New Testament elevates it to the radical love that freely gives and freely receives. We see Jesus telling a rich man to give it *all* to the poor (Matthew 19:21). Freely give. We see Him also praise a woman for lavishing costly perfume on His feet (Mark 14). Freely receive. We see Paul freely ask for gifts of support for fellow believers (1 Corinthians 16). Freely receive. We see the good Samaritan shell out money above and beyond what would be considered normal for a wounded stranger (Luke 10:25–37). Freely give.

The best summation of our mission in finance is this: live open-handed. When your hands are open, your hands are poised to receive. You cannot grasp anything with closed fists. God *wants* to place things in your hands. It is His desire that you have all that you need. He just wants you to rely on His often-unpredictable ways of provision rather than the illusion of security that comes from self-reliant sources. Live open-handed. Open hands also do not hold. Anything that is needed in another place or for another Kingdom purpose that is currently in your hands is available to be redistributed. Do you trust enough to pray about each opportunity to give and receive and then actually respond accordingly?

Full disclosure, I remember being in college and they'd pass the offering plate, and if I dropped something big in there I'd like, "psst...did you see that God? Aren't you proud? I'm really dipping into *my* money to bless you." Wow. I am so thankful for the grace and patience God had in me learning that there is no "my money." It's all always been His anyway! I was guilty of being the third servant! "I work really hard, and you're taking from me!" was my perspective on giving as opposed to realizing *He* is the one who supplies seed to the sower.

The deeper God has taken me on this journey, the more I find that there are so many creative ways to financially support the Kingdom with our gifts. When I say gifts, I'm not talking about tithe. Tithe is tithe, but *gifts* . . . that's the "extra." That's the bonus giving. I don't know if there's any other Shark Tank fans reading this, but just imagine you are a Heavenly shark. The money the Lord has given you—He has given to *you* to manage. And He does so with confidence, not setting you up for an impossible task, but knowing you can do well with it. Yes, we tithe our 10%, but we don't only *manage* 10% of our money. Be strategic and prayerful about what you choose to "partner" your money with. Maybe you're answering God's promptings of being someone's answer to prayer financially this month. Maybe you're purposeful about which stores you support because you want to see Kingdom entrepreneurs be able to further the vision that God put in their hearts. There may not be a one-size-fits-all comprehensive financial plan for everyone, but there is one overarching theme we see throughout Biblical finance from the widow's mite to Solomon's riches. That truth is that the Lord looks at the *heart* behind the gift . . . not the amount. He praised the one with five talents as much as He praised the one with two. Whichever is closer to what's in your hands, pray and ask the Lord for strategic insights on how to do even more financially for His Kingdom. His answers may surprise you.

Talents

The parable is called parable of the talents, denoting a sum of money. How interesting, though, is it to think of actual *talents*. The problem with the word "talent" is that our contemporary culture has injected the word "talent" with the essence of "competition." If you are talented, you're the best. Or one of the best. Or very good in *comparison*. In fact, sometimes we don't know how to "be" without comparison. Not that all comparison is bad. Comparing our lives to the Word of God is a great comparison that can bring life-giving pruning and direction. Usually, though, that's not the kind of comparing we are doing.

When our first child was born, he was a chunky, thriving, beautiful baby boy. With no complications we took him home on the second day. He sped through sizes, wearing sizes for almost twice his age sometimes. I internally thought, "I am just such a great mom. This kid is growing like a weed because *I'm* doing great!"

Then came our daughter. If you recall our five harrowing days in the hospital and trip to the NICU with a suspected (but non-existent) heart condition, you can imagine how I was already eating my words. We took our little baby girl home. And I do mean *little* baby girl. Our doctor calls her "the gymnast" because she's tall and thin—barely hanging on to the 10th percentile in weight. Others would compare her constantly, making comments about her size and asking about her eating habits. I would then agonize over her not being her chunky brother. Is something wrong? Did I do something? Then God spoke profoundly, *"Comparison is the thief of joy."* Her middle name is Joy, and I believe God named her that because that's what He was teaching me about. The enemy was stealing my joy. Why? Because I was comparing. She was perfectly normal—her normal—but I was caught in "weeping and gnashing of teeth" because I was comparing.

I share that because everyone has talents. Talents or skills are easy to dismiss when we don't feel very exceptional *in comparison*. But God doesn't compare. He didn't take the servants and say, "You did good. But not as good as that guy." Nor does he say, "Why can't you be more like him? He's crushing it! You could do better." He simply gives according to the plans *He* has and celebrates good stewardship. Galatians reminds us, "Each one should test their own actions. Then they can take pride in themselves alone, *without comparing* themselves to someone else, for each one should carry their own load." (Gal. 6:4–5).

I challenge you that if you've buried an ability or talent...it's time to go dig it up and invest it. You're still here. You're still part of the global story God is authoring. He didn't give you that talent or skill by accident. Time to ask Him what to do with it.

Time

It's interesting that the verbs used with time imply its value. We *invest* time. We *spend* time. We *waste* time. We *make* time. You could substitute money for time in any of those sentences, and it would fit. Just as we have the tithe for money, we have the Sabbath for time. God saw such value in time that He asks us to set aside one out of seven days for Sabbath.

Time is perhaps one of the most valuable things we are given to steward. Not surprisingly, it's the commodity most under attack these days. We don't have time. We're too busy. We have too much time. We're aimless. What does it look like to invest our time in a way that makes it subordinate to and serving of the Kingdom of God? How do we *multiply* time?

Time is experienced so differently at different times. I taught fitness classes for years, and I *still* can't understand why a minute of doing squats feels like an eternity whereas the two-hour break in my house known as "nap time" lasts what feels like two seconds!

This spring, I was a part of a peer cohort of CEOs from mission organizations throughout the country. This particular meeting, we were discussing the importance of discipleship as a source of growth. Being discipled at all times, and discipling at all times. Surprisingly, I learned that when those in high leadership positions were asked about mentoring. the two most common reasons that keep them from agreeing to mentor are lack of time or not feeling qualified. The second reason ties into what I just said about comparison robbing talents. These were senior level executives that still didn't feel "good enough"! But the first reason is what I want to focus on: time.

Especially in this weird "virtual" world (post 2020), you may not have time with as many people as you used to. I bet, though, that you have time with one. I'm going to tell you a story about one person. On a work trip to check in with partners in Southeast Asia, we visited a farm. We sat around a kitchen table on a hot and muggy jungle morning as the sunlight filtered in the open windows, and a woman told us her testimony through a translator. She has been an animist. She had shrines and believed in and worshiped the "spirits." She took a job at the farm. She actually was pretty bad at it. She just couldn't get the "farm stuff" down, *but* she described to us how the farm manager had grace and offered her instead a job working for his family in their home doing what she loved which was cooking, cleaning, and helping with the kids.

Through the *time* she spent with that family, she was won over by the love of Christ and chose to become a Christian. She burned her alters. She was a already widow, but by converting she was then rejected by the rest of her family. She just had one other friend who was also a widow in the area who had converted too. At that point in the testimony our translator stopped translating. Her eyebrows shot up and she started cross-talking with this woman for several minutes. We were all waiting in suspense, not knowing what was happening. Finally, realizing we were still waiting for the rest of the story, our translator looks at me in disbelief and says, "She says that her and the other woman started meeting as a church, and they are now over two hundred members. They have trouble finding a place to meet. I am in shock."

I honestly don't know if that original farm manager ever knew the ripple effects of his family's time invested in that woman. Nor do I think we fully know the ripple effects of ours. But time, too, is something we can invest, put to work, and watch God multiply the Kingdom. I think it really is as simple as asking God to reveal the time and season you are in. There is a time and season for everything, and certainly God has ideas for yours. Interestingly, we call the clock parts that mark out our day, "hands," so again, I ask: "What is in your *hands*?"

COMPETING FOR OUR PEACE

> *No one can serve two masters. Either you will hate the one*
> *and love the other, or you will be devoted to the one and*
> *despise the other. You cannot serve both God and money.*

Matthew 6:24

Human needs build on each other. The most pressing needs are at the forefront of our attention, and it's almost impossible to focus on anything else until we have the peace that these will be met. In a world where our control is minimal and our foresight is limited, we seek peace in one of two places. We find it in God, or we find it in worldly security. Maybe we find peace in our paycheck. Maybe we find peace in our abilities. Maybe we find peace in our titles. Any of these can changes. We *need* peace in our Provider God.

The above verse in Matthew hits the nail on the head because you cannot seek peace from both God and the world. This doesn't mean anyone *wants* or would sign up for a season of scarcity. Not loving money does *not* mean loving poverty. The Bible very clearly promotes *good stewardship* of whatever amount you have. It doesn't assert poverty as a goal or as pleasing to God. Nor does it present it as a prosperity gospel of whomever has the most is the most pleasing to God. When the shift happens to recognizing God as the giver behind everything that comes in (as opposed to the paycheck itself as being your security), we realize what a gift each provision is regardless of our status. It transforms our mind. We also realize that, day to day, we are living with manna in the desert. Having your needs met is one leap of faith to another, and we never arrive at being our own provider. Even if we seem pretty unshakable. This realization is full of praise and joy! The daily gratitude of knowing that *today* God has *done* something visible to provide for your needs makes you savor these moments. When we see our job or our paycheck as irrevocable or expected, we get comfortable and stop seeing it as God providing. As a result, we reject or resent times when we have to make leaps of financial faith because we have stopped recognizing that every day is a leap. We begin to detest the leap and detest God for making us take it.

The one who chooses God, however, also *does not seek to be poor*. This also is speaking of talents! It does nothing for God for you to belittle your talents, forego your promotion, or live an austere life *unless* He has specifically instructed you to do so. It's easy to read Matthew 6:24 but still not fully grasp the entirety of it and, instead, think that in order to love God well that you must not have or use money. Or that somehow surviving on as little as possible means you're more loved or esteemed by God. That's not what it says. Imagine if all the wealth, talents, titles, and resources of the world went to those who weren't following the Lord. Yikes! There are great possibilities when God's people are stewarding resources and finances well.

The alternative to stewardship (that we see in the parable of the talents) is *burying it in the ground*. Another word for ground is earth. Are you burying what was entrusted to you in *this* world? This isn't just a literal burying, this is any way in which God's resources, talents, titles, or time are dead-ending. It is investing in something that goes no farther than this earthly life and does nothing for the Kingdom. What do you *choose* to invest what you have in? "W*here your treasure, there your heart will be also*" (Matthew 6:21). Said another way, where you invest (your time/talents/titles/resources) you can find your priorities. Are these things being used in a way that invests in His kingdom? Or are these things going to pass away with this earth?

> "*Whatever you do, work at it with all your heart, as working for the Lord, not for human masters, since you know that you will receive an inheritance from the Lord as a reward. It is the Lord Christ you are serving.*"
>
> *Colossians 3:23–24*

TAKE IT TO GOD:

Ask each of these questions one at a time, and wait in the still silence for God's answer. Jot it down!

What people and resources are You highlighting in this season to disciple me?

What people or person are You highlighting for me to disciples this season?

What are financial "talents" that I have buried that You want to use?

How do You want to invest my time so that it multiplies for Your kingdom?

What are skills or titles of mine that have been buried or not invested for your Kingdom?

What is the next step in all of these areas to be able to better steward and multiply for you?

Chapter Seven

TAKE CHANCES,
MAKE MISTAKES,
GET MESSY

Be perfect, therefore, as your heavenly Father is perfect.

MATTHEW 5:48

PERFECTLY IN PROGRESS

FEW VERSES PRICK A cold sweat like Matthew 5:48. Be perfect!?
Does God really command perfection? Breathe a sigh of relief
because the answer is no. In fact, what is lost in translation is
surprisingly revealing about the Father's expectations of us. The
Greek word associated in *Strong's Concordance* with Matthew
5:48's "perfect" is the word, *teleios*[1]. This word encapsulates the
essence of something that is going through the necessary stages
to become full grown. Like an old pirate telescope expanding one
layer at a time towards fullness, it means, essentially, "in progress,"
"in process," or "becoming complete." Now, re-reading Matthew
5:48, how astonishing is it that all God requires is for us to be un-
dergoing the processes that will make us fully mature or will get us

1. Strong, *Strong's Expanded Exhaustive Concordance of the Bible*, 1676.

to our final destination? It's a lot easier order to fill than perfection. It isn't, however, a walk in the park. Anyone who has ever been in the process of something (which I believe should cover us all) knows that it requires *work*, tenacity, and perseverance. Becoming mature spiritually is not all that different than becoming mature physically. Growing up involves a lot of new chances taken, a lot of mistakes in the learning process, and it is anything but clearly defined.

CHANCE AND CIRCUMSTANCE

The children's series *The Magic School bus (1994)* featured a teacher whose catchphrase to encourage her students on new adventures was "Take chances! Make mistakes! Get messy!" As we look at the teachings of Jesus, we are going to see that his advice wasn't far off. The word "chance" is a worldly word. Jesus did many things that we would call "taking chances" that truthfully were not chances in the eyes of Heaven. Jesus took chances and made them circumstances. Chance implies a possibility of something. Circumstance denotes the actual condition or state of things.

Each time He stretched out His hand and commanded that someone be healed, it is the very same as when we stretch out our hands to those whom God has said to heal. As sons and daughters adopted by God and called to do "even greater things" than Jesus (John 14:12), this is our destiny. Jesus didn't see this as taking a chance, though it feels like that because we do not know the outcome. He saw each of these peoples' complete healings as a circumstance *because He was moving in perfect sync with God*. It was a fact. It was going to happen. Not because He declared it, but because He lived in unison with what He saw the Father doing. This is exactly the chance-to-circumstance conversion we see in a renewed mind.

We read Jesus's encounter with the woman at the well in John chapter four and see another bold chance. God had revealed those insights about the woman's past to Jesus. For Jesus, speaking them was the same as us speaking a prophetic word we have received for someone. From an earthly perspective, it was taking a chance. To Jesus, He knew if God said it, it was a factual circumstance, and there was no chance involved.

When we live in cooperation with the Holy Spirit, we take chances all the time. But these chances are never truly chances. We are actively participating in bringing the circumstances of Heaven to earth. When God calls us to, we are called to take similar "chances" to those we see Jesus take in scripture. How do we know? Because we see the disciples walking in the same kind of boldness.

> He replied, "As you enter the city, a man carrying a jar of water will meet you. Follow him to the house that he enters, and say to the owner of the house, 'The Teacher asks: Where is the guest room, where I may eat the Passover with my disciples?' He will show you a large room upstairs, all furnished. Make preparations there." They left and found things just as Jesus had told them. So, they prepared the Passover.

> Luke 22:10–13

Can you imagine today being sent to follow a stranger to his house and ask him to use his guest room for a dinner party? Some of you reading this may have been asked by God to do something just as ridiculous-looking in the eyes of the world. We know from the way scripture progresses that the disciples did it! They took the chance. The chance became circumstance because it all happened "just as Jesus had told them." How would our boldness change if we truly believed that everything in our lives would happen *just as God is telling us*? Jesus is recorded asking people to leave careers, sell their possessions, and even place Him in a higher priority than their own family members. These are rather large chances to take. But once you see the realities Heaven has already declared into your circumstances, it dwarfs these sacrifices into trades that are *so* advantageous it becomes a no-brainer.

> Now a man who was lame from birth was being carried to the temple gate called Beautiful, where he was put every day to beg from those going into the temple courts. When

he saw Peter and John about to enter, he asked them for money. Peter looked straight at him, as did John. Then Peter said, "Look at us!" So, the man gave them his attention, expecting to get something from them. Then Peter said, "Silver or gold I do not have, but what I do have I give you. In the name of Jesus Christ of Nazareth, walk." Taking him by the right hand, he helped him up, and instantly the man's feet and ankles became strong. He jumped to his feet and began to walk. Then he went with them into the temple courts, walking and jumping, and praising God. When all the people saw him walking and praising God.

Acts 3:2–9

In this passage we see Peter and John solo. There was no Jesus physically walking with them, giving them a play-by-play at this point. Their actions, however, tell us God was clearly speaking to them. Commanding someone who has been unable to walk since birth looks like a rather large chance from an earthly perspective. To them, however, they heard the Holy Spirit within them commanding it, so they spoke that circumstance with confidence and watched its reality emerge. If this hasn't happened to you already—get ready. If it has—prepare for more. There will be times in which God speaks clearly, asking you to take that unorthodox chance and speak to a stranger or pray for healing or deliver a message. When that time comes, remember what you are hearing is not the invitation to take a chance, but the declaration of the true circumstances that already exist.

We descend from one of the biggest "chance-takers" of all. To send one's only son down to die in hopes that He can defeat death, win our hearts back to redemption, and save humanity was perhaps the biggest chance this world could imagine. But God knew it was no chance at all. The victory was already won. He just needed the obedience of His Son to live it out so that it became our circumstance. Then after that, God sends those gathered to His service as *sheep* among *wolves*. That's quite risky to entrust your gospel-spreading sheep in a world which you know is crawling with wolves...*unless* you know their success isn't a chance but a certainty. Look at the leaps God is asking you to take from a heavenly perspective. They will begin to look less and less like chances and more and more like exciting opportunities to find out just how much God has already declared is certain.

MISSED TAKE

I love words and how telling they can be. Mistake is one of my favorites. Mistake literally sounds like you are "miss" "taking" something. A "take" can mean an approach. Sometimes our mistakes are *missing* God's *approach* to a situation.

> From that time on Jesus began to explain to his disciples that he must go to Jerusalem and suffer many things at the hands of the elders, the chief priests and the teachers of the law, and that he must be killed and on the third day be raised to life. Peter took him aside and began to rebuke him. "Never, Lord!" he said. "This shall never happen to you!" Jesus turned and said to Peter, "Get behind me, Satan! You are a stumbling block to me; you do not have in mind the concerns of God, but merely human concerns."
> Matthew 16:21–23

Peter probably felt like he must have made a mistake after this rebuke. And he did. In the sense that God's vision for Jesus and the cross did not match Peter's vision for Jesus's life. Many times, we can make the mistake of rebellion, crying "never!" as Peter did, only to realize later that God had a far larger vision in mind. Peter only hears that His friend, this amazing Son of God who was the fulfillment of God's promises, was now going to die. What God sees is that this death *is* the way in which He is going to fulfill the promises. The good news is that Peter's brief rebellion didn't change the cross. Peter did not prevent his own salvation in spite of his "missed take" of what God was doing. If you have been in a season in which you cried "never!" to God or didn't understand His vision—don't worry. Not only are you not alone, but we have this in scripture to remind us that in those situations we can be *assured* that God's ultimate plan—despite how it may look from our perspective—truly is better.

"Take" can also refer to the film term of the way something is visually or audibly recorded (ie recording several "takes" of a scene). Sometimes our mistakes are not having the same vision or words for a particular situation in your life as God does. When a director asks for another take of a scene, it's because what happened in the first take didn't capture his or her vision.

In John chapter eleven, Mary and Martha are distraught at the grave illness of their brother and dear friend of Jesus, Lazarus. When Jesus tarries and arrives four days after Lazarus has died, the sisters clearly did not envision this scene the way God did. They see that all is lost and lament that if Jesus had only put the donkey in third gear, He could have been there in enough time to save him. We know, though, from scriptural clues that Jesus had God's vision for this scene the whole time. He speaks in verse four that "this sickness will not end in death." Even standing outside of the grave, Jesus prays aloud that what is about to happen has been perfectly composed that way *"for the benefit of the people standing here, that they may believe"* (v. 42). The sisters had missed God's take on their brother's situation. God saw it as a win-win. Their brother would live, *and* many would believe because of the miracle that occurred. *They* had envisioned it as a situation in which Jesus would swoop in before the final hour and save the day before Lazarus even died. When He didn't, they assumed it was a failure or hopeless situation. Sometimes our words and actions don't capture God's vision for our life. The good news is that God is a patient director.

An important thing to note is that mistakes are in the eye of the beholder. A renewed mind has God as its director rather than people. Many—myself included—have fallen prey to letting people direct their lives, judge their takes, and decide their mistakes. Imagine how that would have gone for the following Biblical folks.

> While Jesus was in Bethany in the home of Simon the Leper, a woman came to him with an alabaster jar of very expensive perfume, which she poured on his head as he was reclining at the table. When the disciples saw this, they

were indignant. "Why this waste?" they asked. "This perfume could have been sold at a high price and the money given to the poor." Aware of this, Jesus said to them, "Why are you bothering this woman? She has done a beautiful thing to me. Matthew 26:6–10

Imagine you are a disciple. Here comes a woman you know does not have the best track record. By religious standards, she shouldn't even be associating with Jesus. She comes in and makes a big display, pouring expensive perfume all over his feet. You're thinking, "Oh man, she's done it now. Jesus preaches giving to the poor, and this could've been sold for the poor! I mean, isn't that what He told that guy who asked what he could do to enter the kingdom of God? I can't wait to hear the sermon she gets...." Suddenly, *you* get the rebuke! Total shock ensues. Martha can also relate.

As Jesus and his disciples were on their way, he came to a village where a woman named Martha opened her home to him. She had a sister called Mary, who sat at the Lord's feet listening to what he said. But Martha was distracted by all the preparations that had to be made. She came to him and asked, "Lord, don't you care that my sister has left me to do the work by myself? Tell her to help me!"

"Martha, Martha," the Lord answered, "you are worried and upset about many things, but few things are needed— or indeed only one. Mary has chosen what is better, and it will not be taken away from her." Luke 10:38–42

Occasionally, our judgments of mistakes are not actually mistakes at all. God judges from a vantage point that humans cannot even wrap their minds around. The New Testament is littered with references to not making judgments. Mostly because we aren't great at it. Had either of these women heeded the reaction of those around them, they would have felt ashamed. They would have believed they had made mistakes. Depending on who each woman let be the director of her life, she could have felt affirmed or felt ashamed.

Let's say you're having your pastor over for dinner. You're enjoying a wonderful conversation when you hear banging. The din grows louder and louder until—*crash*—a member of your congregation plops through the roof with a friend. As the dust settles on your perfectly prepared casserole, you hear the person apologize and say that his friend just needed prayer, so he wanted to see the pastor. Do you feel like this person made a mistake?

In Luke 5:18–25 this is exactly what happens. A paralytic is lowered through the roof by his friends to receive healing from Jesus. Does Jesus reprimand him? No! And this is before the time of homeowner's insurance! This is an important reminder the next time we begin to judge the way someone else serves or worships God. It's also an important reminder the next time we *feel* judged for the way we are serving or being obedient. From the perspective of the religious culture of the time, much of what Jesus did were mistakes. He healed on the Sabbath, ate with sinners, and confronted the most "righteous" of society about their errors. Is this an excuse for us to do whatever we want—regardless of the opinions of others in our church? Of course not! Our priority is always to love. Our priority is not, however, to people please. The key to making mistakes the *right* way is knowing *who* in your life is defining what is a mistake. If God and His Word truly is your compass, then you may make choices that leave others without a renewed mindset scratching their heads, but you will not be mistaken.

A man I deeply respect who is a business mentor gave me a great piece of advice. He said he asks all his applicants to tell what their biggest mistake on the job has been. If they have no answer, he knows they're probably not ready to work for him. The truth is, most of us would rather hide our blunders. Blunders teach us, though. The first mission organization I ever tried to direct failed. We couldn't recruit enough people and keep them on the field through the pandemic. It took a lot of humility and flexibility to pivot and let go of a dysfunctional model. I learned more from that failure than I could have ever imagined. Don't reject the idea of ever failing. Learn from it when it happens.

Know that we *all* will have misses. That's part of being human. It's part of growing into maturity. Remember our Greek word for perfect is growing into maturity. In that sense, ironically, misses that are learned from are part of perfection. The renewed mind not only knows how to learn from its misses, but it knows how to let God define what is and isn't a miss.

FILTHY FAITHFULNESS

Dusty feet are faithful feet.

> *Go rather to the lost sheep of Israel. As you go, proclaim this message: 'The kingdom of heaven has come near.' Heal the sick, raise the dead, cleanse those who have leprosy, drive out demons. Freely you have received; freely give.*
>
> Matthew 10:6–8

I picture the disciples listening to these words wide-eyed, their hearts brimming with anticipation and expectation of what they would see and do. Immediately after this triumphant send off, Jesus instructs,

> *If anyone will not welcome you or listen to your words, leave that home or town and shake the dust off your feet.*
>
> Matthew 10:14

How many of us want to "go" but don't want to get our feet dirty? Not only did Jesus get His feet dirty, but He got down and took the dirty, grimy feet of others in His hands and washed them. Jesus healed blindness by rubbing spit dirt on someone's face (Matt. 7:33). He made a mess at the temple flipping tables over (Matt. 21:12), and touched dead bodies to bring complete healing (widow's son, Jairus' daughter, and Lazarus).

Selling out for the kingdom of God may find you in some messy places. It may bring you to dirt floors. It may bring you to people with festering wounds needing healing. If not physically messy, following Christ won't always be without its emotional messes. It will be sitting with people in crisis, feeling the mess of betrayal, and having attacks that muddy the waters of life.

> *"Do not suppose that I have come to bring peace to the earth. I did not come to bring peace, but a sword. For I have come to turn "a man against his father, a daughter against her mother, a daughter-in-law against her mother-in-law—a man's enemies will be the members of his own household."*
>
> *Matthew 10:34-36*

It's important to note that Jesus never negated that we love or pray for our enemies. He did say that we will be "turned against" which simply means not aligned with. While our mission is to love, our following Christ will guarantee that we will be at odds with others in this world. Sometimes those others may be very close to us. God tells us this not to scare us, but to reassure us that if we do receive hostility for our faith—it's *normal!*

In fact, in Matthew chapter thirteen, our quest for God's kingdom is compared to buried treasure. Treasure that's hidden in a field is not visible. It's buried beneath the muck of dirt and bugs and old leaves. Only when we dive into this mess with both hands, knowing the treasure below is well worth it, do we lay our hands on the kingdom of heaven. The man in the parable dug through the dirt not once but twice! He completely sold everything he owned to do so. Unless the man found it the first time, he could not have been certain it was there. It took faith and digging in the mess to find it. I encourage you—literally, metaphorically, however God is calling you—to get messy! The best treasures are buried beneath the dirt.

> *"The kingdom of heaven is like treasure hidden in a field. When a man found it, he hid it again, and then in his joy went and sold all he had and bought that field."*
>
> *Matthew 13:44*

TAKE IT TO GOD:

Ask each of these questions one at a time, and wait in the still silence for God's answer. Jot it down!

How am I "perfect" in progress right now to You?

What chances are you calling me to take this season?

What miss-takes are you looking to correct in my heart and mind this season?

How do You want to get messier in my ministry to the lost around me?

Chapter Eight

LEVEL GROUND

For God does not show favoritism.

ROMANS 2:11

LEVEL-LESS

THIS WORLD—AND OUR HUMAN minds—are full of levels. For proof, just look at all we create. We create jobs with levels, education with levels, even games are created with levels. All these levels are solely based on *achievement*. Levels in themselves are not entirely bad. We have scriptural references to a few distinctions in levels of power such as:

> *You made them [referencing man] a little lower than the angels; you crowned them with glory and honor.*
>
> *Hebrews 2:7*
>
> *Then God said, "Let us make mankind in our image, in our likeness, so that they may rule over the fish in the sea and the birds in the sky, over the livestock and all the wild animals, and over all the creatures that move along the ground."*
>
> *Genesis 1:26*

*I have given you authority to trample on snakes and scor-
pions and to overcome all the power of the enemy; nothing
will harm you.*

Luke 10:19

We have been given authority. We are lower than God, and
we are far more powerful than the enemy and his forces. The
lies creep in when we feel that we can be on different Heavenly
levels from *each other* due to our own achievement. We confuse
being *set apart* for God's purposes as being *set above* others for
God's purposes. When we impose these levels—both in how we
view ourselves and in how we view others—we place limits on our
thinking. *God wants us to be limitless in our love which requires us
being level-less in our thinking.* This is part of the renewed mind.

Have you ever underestimated someone? During a homeless
ministry we came across a man who was in serious need of medical care for a broken ankle. As I try to communicate his needs and
direct people, one of the women with us bends down and starts
speaking to him about what happened with his ankle. Frustrated, I
thought to myself "I just asked him. I can speak Spanish too. What
makes you think you're better?" To my surprise, even though I had
worked with her the entire trip, I found out then and there that she
was nurse. That knowledge immediately made me hand over the
lead to her on this situation because she was trained and qualified
in a way that I wasn't. Had I never found that out, I would have
looked foolish trying to take the lead when someone who knew far
better than I was available to help.

Have you ever been underestimated? Being on either side of
these situations (underestimating and being underestimated) has
taught me something valuable: God sees so much differently than
we do because *His* knowledge is complete. When God chooses
someone for something, He does so because He knows something.
If we knew all that God did, we would likely feel silly about our
grumblings. Often, we underestimate His knowledge as well as
underestimate each other.

> *But the Lord said to Samuel, "Do not consider his appearance or his height, for I have rejected him. The Lord does not look at the things people look at. People look at the outward appearance, but the Lord looks at the heart."*

1 Samuel 16:7

It's impossible to meet someone and instantly know his or her story, training, wisdom, anointings, callings, and giftings, Everyone has these things though. The combination of all our experience, wisdom, anointings, and giftings makes us so strong as the body of Christ. We won't know everyone's complete story. How then can we be level-less? The best answer has been modeled by Jesus himself:

> *"Jesus called them together and said, "You know that the rulers of the Gentiles lord it over them, and their high officials exercise authority over them. Not so with you. Instead, whoever wants to become great among you must be your servant, and whoever wants to be first must be your slave— just as the Son of Man did not come to be served, but to serve, and to give his life as a ransom for many."*

Matthew 20:25–28

Jesus, being perfectly connected to the Father, really did have more wisdom than everyone around Him. *He still charges us to forego lording our qualifications for humility.* Jesus doesn't say, however, to forego your *spiritual authority*. We use our spiritual authority to make declarations, defeat the powers of darkness, and confidently walk in the way of the Lord. We *don't* use our spiritual authority, however, to lord over people. The more spiritual leadership roles you take on, the more you will find yourself serving. Those of you in leadership currently reading this are laughing at the truth of it. Paul knew this well. He writes about it in his letter to the Philippians, telling them how he has chosen to sacrifice all the prestige his accomplishments could have gotten him because he knows he too was saved by faith and not works.

> *If someone else thinks they have reasons to put confidence in the flesh, I have more: circumcised on the eighth day,*

*of the people of Israel, of the tribe of Benjamin, a Hebrew
of Hebrews; in regard to the law, a Pharisee; as for zeal,
persecuting the church; as for righteousness based on the
law, faultless.*

*But whatever were gains to me I now consider loss for the
sake of Christ. What is more, I consider everything a loss
because of the surpassing worth of knowing Christ Jesus
my Lord, for whose sake I have lost all things. I consider
them garbage, that I may gain Christ and be found in him,
not having a righteousness of my own that comes from the
law, but that which is through faith in Christ—the righteousness that comes from God on the basis of faith.*

Philippians 3:4b-9

I joined a nine-month cohort group a few years ago geared to
grow its participant in CEO Leadership. Ironically, the entire first
half of the course was not swapping trade secrets, finding shortcuts, or gaining skills. It was focusing on Jesus's servant leadership.
That's all. The amount of relevance that Jesus's servant leadership
example has on how we ran our organizations was astounding.
Truly, the greater leadership capacity you are elevated to, the more
serving you can expect to do. Even when you're at the "top" in the
eyes of the world, you can see through Christ that these "levels"
mean nothing compared to the posture of your heart.

Because we are all saved by faith, it is beautiful level ground
we all stand on. Everyone is saved through faith in Christ. No person is "more saved" because it's not works-based. Also, since it isn't
earned, the only response we can have to this great gift is serving
God with a full heart. The next time you find yourself feeling better than—or lesser than—someone else, ask yourself, "What does
God know about this person that I don't?". More than likely, they
have more than what you can see. We are all equalized by grace.
We are all united in loving God. We must remind ourselves that
regardless of how we *feel* about them, our job is to serve as Jesus
served.

*For by the grace given me I say to every one of you: Do not
think of yourself more highly than you ought, but rather*

*think of yourself with sober judgment, in accordance with
the faith God has distributed to each of you.*

Romans 12:3

HUMBLE—NOT CRUMBLE

An important distinction in serving how Jesus served is that Jesus did not serve people in order to put Himself underneath them. He served because God had called Him to love them, so His service was putting God at the top—not putting those *people* at the top. There is an important difference between positioning yourself to serve others verses positioning people in the place of masters or gods. Jesus serving was a sacrifice of pride. He was telling God that doing His will—serving and love—was more important than needing to feel more important than other people.

Many of us, at one time or another, mistake humble for crumble. We have that moment of feeling so unworthy, feeling so less-than, and feeling like everyone around us is better. Even worse, we feel like that's how we *should* feel. We feel called to make ourselves nothing and serve others as *better than* ourselves. We twist this self-abasement into feeling like holiness. God, however, did not call us to love others as *better than* ourselves. He called us to love others *as* ourselves.

> *Jesus replied: "'Love the Lord your God with all your heart
> and with all your soul and with all your mind.¹ This is the
> first and greatest commandment. And the second is like it:
> 'Love your neighbor as yourself.'*
>
> Matthew 22:37–39

The motivation or goal behind humility is making God more and equalizing others and ourselves. A side effect of making God more prominent than our self-seeking flesh will be serving others. It means giving our life to be used by God rather than giving our life to be used for our own purposes, but the motivation or goal was never to make ourselves nothing. You are far from nothing to God, and He paid the highest price to get you back!

> *For you know that it was not with perishable things such as silver or gold that you were redeemed from the empty way of life handed down to you from your ancestors, but with the precious blood of Christ, a lamb without blemish or defect.*

1 Peter 1:18–19

Imagine you loved someone dearly. To help that person out and get out of debt, you offered to pay all they owed. This included paying off a $150,000 mortgage on that person's house. Afterwards, to show gratitude, that person tells you they were never worth that gift, so they felt unworthy to live in the house and have been living on the streets. What!? Your heart behind giving was to show love, and your gift was not motivated by that person "earning it" or being "worthy." It also would be an insult to your judgment. It's as if they are saying, "you judged poorly and spent your money foolishly."

God paid a far higher price for you. God, in fact, paid the *highest* price. Treating yourself as below others or unworthy is like calling Him foolish for paying such a high price for you. Trust me. God is no fool. He didn't pay different prices for different people. He paid one price for all. This sets the level ground that we should stand on side by side. Do not disqualify yourself from the sonship that God has called you to and insist on persisting as a slave.

PRIDE VS CONFIDENCE

Squinting through the window, the old man's heart skips a beat. "Could it be?" he wonders tentatively. "No," he scolds himself, dismissing his hope, "It's been too long. My old eyes are playing tricks on me." Yet there it was. The mirage didn't fade. The muddied and ragged feet of the prodigal son plodding up the road towards his father's house.

This prodigal son from Luke chapter fifteen is the approach many of us take. As the son trudges back, his head is filled with all his failures and shortcomings. More than likely, he's comparing himself to his brother, feeling far inferior. He returns hoping only to be a slave.

> I will set out and go back to my father and say to him: Father, I have sinned against heaven and against you. I am no longer worthy to be called your son; make me like one of your hired servants.' So, he got up and went to his father.

> "But while he was still a long way off, his father saw him and was filled with compassion for him; he ran to his son, threw his arms around him and kissed him.

> "The son said to him, 'Father, I have sinned against heaven and against you. I am no longer worthy to be called your son.'

> "But the father said to his servants, 'Quick! Bring the best robe and put it on him. Put a ring on his finger and sandals on his feet. Bring the fattened calf and kill it. Let's have a feast and celebrate. For this son of mine was dead and is alive again; he was lost and is found.' So, they began to celebrate.

> Luke 15:18–24

The father's response is identical to our Father's response. You are not a slave. You are a son. You are equal even with those that *seem* perfect and to have never gone astray (like the older brother). The humility it took to return, confessing his wrongs and admitting his unworthiness, is heart-rending in the sight of the Father. He throws His arms around our humility and restores us. The son swallowed his pride, so the father's response is, "Have confidence." Would the father's reaction have been the same if the prodigal son had returned claiming he had done nothing wrong or deserved the highest place of honor? It's an interesting question for which I don't have the answer. What I do know is God—and people made in His image—love a humble heart.

Scoffing and ducking back into the shadow of the stable, the older brother must have been fuming. Years of mucking out stalls and consoling his grief-stricken father have come to a head. He had been cleaning up his brother's mess and picking up his slack since he left. Certainly, his prodigal brother wasn't going to be given an equal spot to him. Was he?

> *"The older brother became angry and refused to go in. So, his father went out and pleaded with him. But he answered his father, 'Look! All these years I've been slaving for you and never disobeyed your orders. Yet you never gave me even a young goat so I could celebrate with my friends. But when this son of yours who has squandered your property with prostitutes comes home, you kill the fattened calf for him!'*
>
> *"'My son,' the father said, 'you are always with me, and everything I have is yours. But we had to celebrate and be glad, because this brother of yours was dead and is alive again; he was lost and is found.'"*

Luke 15:28–32

I love the Father's equally loving and gentle response to this son. He doesn't rebuke him for being selfish. I don't even hear him raising his voice when I read this. In fact, I hear the father—I hear *our* Father—with a gentle compassion. The meaning behind his words says one thing clearly: have confidence. Be humble. How interesting that this is the message to both brothers. Be humble, but have confidence. The brothers stand on *level ground.*

How do we have confidence without it crossing over the gray line into pride? The prodigal son came back to his father for provision. He approached with confidence, being assured not of his own merit but of the compassion he knew was characteristic of his dad. God wants us to have *confidence.* Not in our own merit, but in His characteristics to save, to love, and to overcome. When we hold ourselves in front of others with the *confidence* of being a loved son or daughter, suddenly we're not jockeying for their approval or caught up in our shortcomings. Suddenly our message and actions become not our own. We get a supernatural confidence that comes from going on behalf of the Lord.

This confidence was the remedy the heart of the older brother needed. If he could truly understand that all His father had was his *and that the other son was not going to take any of it away from him*, he would have had the confidence and security to welcome him in love. The opposite of confidence is insecurity. When we aren't confident, we don't feel secure. For something to be secure, it is fixed, safe, or unchanging. It cannot be taken away. Isn't this deep-down the root of many of our emotional outbursts? We fear having what we feel is ours taken away. God tells you that all He has is yours despite whether you're more like the prodigal son or the older brother. His love is yours. His approval is yours. His resources are yours. His authority is yours. This is the confidence and security we are to walk in.

Merriam Webster defines *pride,* (as opposed to confidence), as "a feeling of happiness that you get when you or someone you know does something good, difficult, etc." The word "achievements" makes all the difference. Pride—or lack thereof—inserts itself in the context of merit. Pride is a false confidence. It *seems* like confidence, but the central point is *us* instead of God. If confidence is security in God's character and abilities, pride is *false* security in our character and abilities. Because it hinges on achievements, pride can swing either way. When we've done well, we feel exalted above those who haven't (much like the older brother). When we've messed up, we feel beneath those who have done better (much like the prodigal son). There is no level ground in pride. In fact, all we need to know about the level ground the Lord desires for us is locked inside the word prodigal itself. Many assume it means "wayward" or "repentant." It means closer to "extravagant" or "lavish." While the son may have also been prodigal in his reckless spending, the whole story actually describes a prodigal *father*. A father who extravagantly lavishes his love and resources *equally* on *both* sons as each of them learn to humbly walk out their sonship.

In him we have redemption through his blood, the forgive-
ness of sins, in accordance with the riches of God's grace that
he lavished on us. With all wisdom and understanding

Ephesians 1:7–8

TAKE IT TO GOD:

Ask each of these questions one at a time, and wait in the still silence for God's answer. Jot it down!

In what ways have I embraced false humility that is actually
interfering with what you want to do through me?

In what area(s) do you want to build confidence?

Where is my pride getting in the way?

In what situations have I thought of myself on a different "level"
than others? Give me eyes to see without levels.

Chapter Nine

NINETY-NINE TO ONE-OF-A-KIND

What do you think? If a man owns a hundred sheep, and one of them wanders away, will he not leave the ninety-nine on the hills and go to look for the one that wandered off?

MATTHEW 18:12

CRUNCHING NUMBERS

FROM CUSTOMERS TO CONNECTIONS on social media, the numbers game pervades our society. There's a certain power or mass perceived in having many. In the process of renewing the mind, God takes us from crunching numbers to crunching the *need* for numbers. Scripture turns our understanding of the power of numbers upside down. In the eyes of Heaven, less truly is more.

Gideon gives me hope. When we meet him in Judges chapter six, he's threshing wheat as he's *hiding* in the wine press because he doesn't want to be discovered by the Midianites. An angel appears to him. Let's let that sink in. An *angel* appears to him. Can you imagine just pulling weeds in your backyard when all of a sudden, an angel appears to you? This angel greets him saying, "The Lord is with you mighty warrior!" (v 12). He is hiding, yet heaven calls him a mighty warrior. Now, just to make sure they didn't get the wrong address, he reminds God that he's from the smallest, weakest tribe and is the least qualified in his family. God assures him he is chosen and will take down every last Midianite.

Fast forward to battle time. Gideon has gathered a huge troop of 32,000 men. If I were Gideon, I would've expected God to say, "I've chosen you for this victory, so I'm going to make sure you have overwhelming reinforcements to take down the enemy." Instead, at the last minute, God comes back and tells him he has too many men. God asks him to send home all who don't want to fight. To fight or not to fight? Duh! That's a no-brainer. Those who take him up on the offer are *twenty-two thousand*. You know Gideon had to be sweating and silently congratulating himself on being obedient through that difficult order. God had one more elimination round in store. He takes Gideon's troops from the original thirty-two thousand to just *three hundred*. And they *win*. Because God never intended the story to read that brave Gideon assembled a massive army on behalf of the Lord which would make victory obvious. God wanted the story to show how *only* God could have pulled off a massive victory under those conditions. The renewed mind doesn't calculate the odds. It knows it only needs one (Almighty God) on its side to win.

THE TWELVE

Ever have those moments where you are just done with people? I saw an internet meme that was all-too-relatable that made me chuckle. It read; "If you're reading this out there—God's not done with you! . . . But I am." There are just those times you are over "*people-ing*". You keep your head down in the supermarket hoping not to have to engage in conversation. At the office you shut the door to give a hint that you don't want company. All you moms out there spending extra time in the bathroom just for the peace and quiet, I'm with you sister! Jesus could relate too. He'd take off to the mountain or push off in a boat sometimes just to escape the crowds. He had no shortage of people vying for His time and attention. And it would be rude, even downright ungodly, to refuse any of them His time, compassion, or attention . . . right? After all, He was Jesus! Actually, we see a very different model.

God could have moved Jesus's heart to minister to the masses, seeking out the bustling cities on purpose and choosing the most public opportunities. It *is* true that He did preach to the masses at times, and this was a very good thing. The miraculous fish and loaves happened at a teaching to thousands. The day to day, however, was spent in a much more strategic way. He did not choose thousands. He didn't even choose the three hundred that Gideon had. He chose twelve. Twelve people out of the thousands. Why? Love is not felt in the masses. The lie of the world is that we will feel love in the masses. Superstars can attest that even with widespread fame, loneliness prevails. We think if we had more friends, more fame, more clients, more people in our lives that we would be happier. But love is intimate. Intimacy requires a figurative close space. And just like your space in the natural, the spiritual space close to you is limited. Love chooses the one out of the ninety-nine. It is in our close circles—whether they are circles of two or circles of twenty—that we have relationships that are the most impactful. God did not choose the twelve *over* choosing the masses. He chose the twelve *in order to* reach the masses. He knew that through meaningful, intentional, personal relationship that He would sow into these twelve who would then sow into dozens more who would eventually ripple out into what is still going on today: the Great Commission. The renewed mind asks God to reveal the *one* who needs love rather than pursuing the ninety-nine that we think will make us *feel* loved.

TINY BEGINNINGS

Hearing the phrase "the kingdom of heaven" simultaneously triggers vast quantities of images and no specific image at the same time. God knows this is a hard concept for us to wrap our minds around, so He gives us a few images from His heart in scripture.

He told them another parable: "The kingdom of heaven is like a mustard seed, which a man took and planted in his field. Though it is the smallest of all seeds, yet when it grows, it is the largest of garden plants and becomes a tree, so that the birds come and perch in its branches."

He told them still another parable: "The kingdom of heaven is like yeast that a woman took and mixed into about sixty pounds of flour until it worked all through the dough."

"Again, the kingdom of heaven is like a merchant looking for fine pearls. When he found one of great value, he went away and sold everything he had and bought it.

Matthew 13:31–33, 45–46

A mustard seed, a tiny bit of yeast, and a single pearl all have one thing in common. They are small. With all of these things, though, massive changes are made. The mustard seed grows into "the largest of the garden plants." The yeast works its way through the entire batch of flour. The pearl had worth that was more massive than the summation of everything else the merchant owned. God's point is simple, and it is mind-transforming. It doesn't take something big to do something big. Sure, sometimes God parts the Red Sea. That's pretty massive. More often, God does things that appear smaller, but the changes caused are more massive and valuable than the "big things" ever could be.

WHAT "COUNTS"

Ok, so if numbers don't count, then what does count to God? What does He see great value and opportunity in? Let's look again at the book of clues God left us to discovering Him, His love, and His plans—*The Bible.*

In Luke 7 when the sinful woman anoints the feet of Jesus with costly perfume, we have an interesting window into the way Heaven sees value. Simon very pragmatically points out that *many poor people* (again he's thinking numbers and masses) could have been helped if this perfume had been sold as opposed to "wasting" it on the feet of only one. Jesus is quick to correct.

> " Then he turned toward the woman and said to Simon, "Do you see this woman? I came into your house. You did not give me any water for my feet, but she wet my feet with her tears and wiped them with her hair. You did not give me a kiss, but this woman, from the time I entered, has not stopped kissing my feet. You did not put oil on my head, but she has poured perfume on my feet. Therefore, I tell you, her many sins have been forgiven—as her great love has shown. But whoever has been forgiven little loves little.""
>
> Luke 7:44–47

He makes an interesting point that her genuine passion to love one outweighed the potential monetary blessing that could've helped (in a more removed way) many. Much can be done with little involvement of the heart. One could throw a massive charity effort and feed hundreds with little heart involvement. One could give a grandiose financial gift to charity with little heart involvement. It is the *change in her heart towards love* that prompts this sacrifice. Love is what matters. Love is what "counts" to God. Love is what changes hearts. It isn't how many people you touched, but how many did you truly and deeply relationship with? It isn't how much you gave but what kind of heart with which you gave.

NOT HOLDING BACK

If you've ever hung out at the food court of an amusement park, you've witnessed the sweaty, whiney, "hanger" (hunger and anger-induced restlessness) that gets hold of a crowd that has had too much sun and too little food. Imagine over five thousand like this. Now take away the food court. No food for miles and miles.

> As evening approached, the disciples came to him and said, "This is a remote place, and it's already getting late.

> Send the crowds away, so they can go to the villages and
> buy themselves some food."
>
> Matthew 14:15

Again, the disciples were doing the math. A quick glance
told them that there were too many people to feed. Have you been
there? Has God put a dream in your heart that you think, "there's
no way I have enough to do that"? God has a history of moving
when the numbers don't add up. Jumping over to the synoptic ac-
count in John, we continue.

> Philip answered him, "It would take more than half a year's
> wages to buy enough bread for each one to have a bite!"
>
> Another of his disciples, Andrew, Simon Peter's brother,
> spoke up, "Here is a boy with five small barley loaves and
> two small fish, but how far will they go among so many?"
>
> John 6:7–8

Jesus wasn't doing a headcount. He also wasn't tabulating a
budget like Philip. Aren't these the first things that we count? We
count the cost. Now, we aren't told much about this boy. No doubt
he was hungry too. If it were me, I may have stealthily hidden my
snack and high-tailed it out of there. Giving food when you are
hungry is among the hardest things to do. Now, let's expand that
beyond food. Giving away anything that you are hungry for is difficult. This is the personification of "not my will but yours be done."
This boy's will more than likely was to eat. Him surrendering his
lunch was surrendering that will to whatever Jesus had in mind.
That takes trust! That is what counts to God. It was not about how
many baskets were left over, how much money they saved, or how
big the crowd was. It was about whether they (the boy and the
disciples) would submit their will, their logic, and their numbers
to God in trust. When the numbers are just numbers to you, you
open the floodgates of abundance.

My guess from knowing the heart of God through the rest
of scripture is that He designed us and Him to have a relationship
that has nothing held back. It is supposed to be characterized by

raw intimacy and breath-to-breath closeness. When Adam and Eve lied and held knowledge back from the Lord about what they had done, death made its first entrance. Ananias and Sapphira are New Testament examples of holding back and how it's still a dead end. We need to hold nothing back. I think that includes even being honest with God when we're at a place in which we're not ready yet to hold nothing back. I believe He has grace for that. He works with that because there is a *willingness*. But when we even withhold our vulnerability and honesty from Him, there is little ground for trust to be grown.

> For if the willingness is there, the gift is acceptable according to what one has, not according to what one does not have.
>
> 2 Corinthians 8:12

OUTSTANDING

"Why are there 99 leaves?" she asked wrinkling her nose. We were facilitating a kid's Bible study and were talking about worship songs. Specifically, the song *Reckless Love* came up. In the song it sings of how God chases down and fights for each of us as His chosen one. One line even references the shepherd in Matthew 18:12 that leaves the ninety-nine other sheep to search for the lost sheep. This night one of my favorite kids, the spunkier of the bunch, was asking why it sang about ninety-nine leaves (gesturing her hands like tree leaves falling). I laughed and said, "Oh no, it says leaves. Like walks away from." Her eyes widened.

"*Leaves*? Why would He leave?!" she asked.

I smiled and replied, "Because he loves you enough *to go after you when you do*."

Being the One

How many girls have been enthralled by stories like *Cinderella*? A prince scouring the land for one girl because she was so irreplaceable. We ache for the kind of love that says we are irreplaceable. This is why we often talk about finding a spouse as finding "the one." As the bride of Christ, for Him *we are the one.* He tells all the angels, "hey...look at that one...that's the one for Me." How many people, similarly, watch movies like *Star Wars* (a current obsession for our son) and long for a role like that in real life. Being the "chosen one" or destined one has this exciting importance to it. We don't just want to be irreplaceable in how we are loved. We want to be irreplaceable in *who we are and what we do.*

When you truly embrace—not at just an academic level, but at a heart-felt, experiential level—what it means to be "the one" for God, there is a transformation that occurs in the mind. *You cannot love and seek the one out of ninety-nine if you have not been sought as the one out of ninety-nine.* We were *made* to be loved this way. This is why that longing persists despite the voices of the world that clamor against it. The world says, "how could you possibly be important in a world of billions of people?" or "you're replaceable and dispensable." The glaring truth, however, is that God could have made a million more people that were carbon copies of you, but He chose to make one unique you. It proves your importance in the billions. You are the *one* who was made to be you. No one can do what you are called to do. No one can love God the way you were designed to love Him. No one can have quite the same relationship that you share with Him. You are the only one in all of time. When you grasp (and I don't even say fully grasp because that's a tall, potentially impossible, order) this love, you will understand what it means to then love others as the one-of-a-kind creation that *they* are too.

LOVING FIRST

I would venture that God created so many of us so that—in His perfectly intended design—together every person can simultaneously be used by Him to *seek out* others with His love while also receiving His love from others He sent to *seek us out*. That doesn't always happen because our world is not the Eden He originally designed. Sometimes we *feel* very alone or unsought. This doesn't change that God's love is passionately seeking us. *Not feeling loved doesn't change the fact that we are the recipients of God's love.* So then just because we feel lonely or unseen, does that mean we stop giving out His love to others? It shouldn't. That actually multiplies the problem (even though it's the very thing we most feel like doing when we feel unloved). I want you to hear this. The reason we love *first*—*before* we feel loved or sought by others—as opposed to loving as a *response* to feeling loved by others, is because God's love always loves first.

> We love because he first loved us.
>
> *1 John 4:19*

Love isn't a feeling. Love is a calling. More than that, love is a commandment. It's how others distinguish us as His people in this world.

> "*You have heard that it was said, 'Love your neighbor and hate your enemy.' But I tell you, love your enemies and pray for those who persecute you, that you may be children of your Father in heaven. He causes his sun to rise on the evil and the good, and sends rain on the righteous and the unrighteous. If you love those who love you, what reward will you get? Are not even the tax collectors doing that? And if you greet only your own people, what are you doing more than others? Do not even pagans do that?*"
>
> *Matthew 5:43–47*

God didn't (and still doesn't) love us because we loved Him first. His love is not a response to Him *feeling* loved by us. He doesn't give us blessings or make sure we have what we need as a reward for loving Him. He sends provision to those who love Him *and* those who don't. If we do the same—if we love *first*—we are different than the world. If we send provision and pray blessing to those who don't love us, we are different from the world. Loving first is a function of the transformed mind. It's not natural, but neither are the supernatural changes that loving first causes.

LOOKING FOR THE ONE

How do we look for the one? In truth, all of us are the one. All of us are unique and precious to Him. All of us move His heart to go after us. Going after every person in the world, however, is not a task we can do or at least not one that we can do well. So why not start with one at a time?

Is someone showing up repeatedly in your dreams? Is someone coming to mind who you haven't thought of in ages? Does your heart feel especially tender towards a certain person? Is God highlighting to you someone who needs help, yet you watch person after person pass by without helping? All of these and more can be "stop signs." Stop signs are when God is trying wildly to get your attention to stop for the one. All of us see these stop signs. The challenge is not rationalizing them away. Usually we take notice, but it's easy to let those seeds be eaten before they're even planted. Seed-eating thoughts assume these things are coincidence, shrink in fear at the thought of the reaction of the individual, or think first of the effort/time/money required to stop.

My challenge is this: Next time you notice a stop sign, stop for the one. Pray and ask God to move your heart toward what *He* is wanting you to do. Maybe it's praying for the person. Maybe it's reaching out with an encouraging word. Maybe it's giving him or her a gift. *It's important to ask God and not assume.* God put him or her on your heart for a reason. It's best to find out what that reason is. When you come to God and ask in prayer to move you to action, be ready. Pay attention to the "go signs" from the Holy Spirit that will follow.

Stopping for the one may be inconvenient or uncomfortable, but God is not asking us to do anything that He hasn't done. In fact, He stops for the one throughout scripture. When Moses was spared in the mass execution of boys his age, God was stopping for the one. When God answered Hannah's prayer for a child, God was stopping for the one. When Jesus turned to answer one specific plea for healing out of a whole crowd that cried out, that was stopping for the one. The entire Bible is a love story about how the God of creation thought that one person was worth everything. And that one person is you.

> For God so loved the world that he gave his one and only Son, that whoever believes in him shall not perish but have eternal life.
>
> John 3:16

TAKE IT TO GOD:

Ask each of these questions one at a time, and wait in the still silence for God's answer. Jot it down!

Where is an area that you want me to focus less on the numbers?

What are some of the things that are unique and wonderful about the way you made me that make me part of the Body of Christ, "the one" for you?

How can I grow in stopping for the one?

Who is one person I have knowingly or unknowingly stopped for that has been a part of something good you've done or are doing?

Chapter Ten

LOCATION, VOCATION, GESTATION

Heaven and earth will pass away, but my words will never pass away.

But about that day or hour no one knows, not even the angels in heaven, nor the Son, but only the Father. As it was in the days of Noah, so it will be at the coming of the Son of Man.

MATTHEW 24:35-37

DIVINE APPOINTMENTS

IMAGINE GOD SENT YOU an invitation. Every party invitation contains a few necessary details. It says where you need to be, what time and date you need to be there, and what the event is that is happening. Occasionally our callings, or invitations, from God come with all of this information, but *way* more often than not, when we receive a calling there are blanks left on our invitations. Why? If God wants us to do something with Him at a certain place and point in time, wouldn't He clearly give us all the information at one time so that we can be sure to make our divine appointments?

That's just it. When we have too much information—or when we *think* we have information that's really incorrect—we try to *make* our divine appointments come together. By trying to make them happen as we think they should, we do more to get more in the way than we do to actually help make them happen. I know that if, in the natural, I received an invitation in the mail that had a blank or two, I wouldn't just guess about the missing details and hope I was right. You wouldn't think, "Hmm..I got an invite to Brad's birthday, but it doesn't say time and date. I'll just try going next Tuesday at noon and see what happens." Yet so often we do just that spiritually. We see missing pieces about God's timing or God's calling, and we try to fill in the gaps ourselves. The problem with this is that God operates on a level that is greater than what we could imagine. In our hasty guesses (or said differently, our imaginations), we often end up filling in the blanks incorrectly.

Using the analogy again of receiving an invitation with blanks, I also wouldn't throw the invitation away and pretend I had never received it. This is another thing we tend to do spiritually out of frustration. Because we don't understand what we are being called to do or where we are supposed to go or what the timing is, we throw out the whole invitation completely, chalking it up to mishearing God.

You know what most of us would do if we received a physical invitation in the mailbox with missing information? We would reach out to the *sender* and ask them to fill in the blanks for us. Spiritually, this is the answer as well. We know of God's character that He *loves* for us to seek Him. He delights in being sought. From God's perspective, these blanks are like little invitations in themselves to spend time with Him, seeking those answers we don't yet have. It's His joy to reveal them. While not having all the answers at one time may be frustrating, it keeps the conversation open. God may give you an appointed time, but you may have no idea what's supposed to happen in that time. God may call you to do a certain thing, but you may have no idea when or where it's going to happen. God may move you to a particular place, but you may have no idea why.

These invitations are the greatest faith *makers* or faith *breakers* in life. The difference between these invitations making your faith or breaking your faith all lies in our *understanding* of them.

Let me first diffuse anxiety by saying *don't worry about missing your divine appointments.* The invitation Sender sends invitations because He *wants* you to come. He does not invite you and then change His mind. He does not leave your divine appointments contingent on you solving them without help. If you have blanks, the answer to filling them in is one of three things: move, wait, or check your compass. Said another way, spiritually investing in a calling takes alignment in location, gestation, or vocation.

LOCATION: THE MOVE

Realtors will always tell you that the value of a property lies primarily in its location. "Location, location, location," the saying goes. There's a lot of spiritual truth to that as well. You can have a gorgeous, well-built structure that's sitting atop a sink hole or landfill which renders it useless. When you put the effort into pursuing a calling (much like putting effort into building something), you want to make sure you're building in the right location.

Recently my husband and I were looking over a survey for a building our church was planning. The architect was explaining the different areas on the survey and why they were important. There were areas that were property lines that we couldn't build within a certain distance of. There were areas that the city used for utility pole lines that we couldn't cross without risking the city tearing down the building. There were sloping areas and flood plains and size of the space all needing consideration when deciding where to place the building. The most striking thing about viewing this survey, is that without a bird's eye view and special, accurate tools, one would never be able to know this information from simply viewing the property. This is a lot like God's view versus our view. God holds the survey of our lives. He knows what has been delegated as our territory or inheritance. He knows where the level ground is. He knows where the flood planes are. He knows what areas risk tearing down our hard work in the future. He knows what features are going to make the build cost us more versus an easier way of building. He also knows the size of what He is building in our lives.

God gives us a specific "where" because He alone knows where can best suit what He is building through us.

A friend of mine had just moved into a new house. A group of us were coming over for a housewarming party. One friend comes in late, her face bright red. Through her laughter she tells us that she got the address wrong and had gone next door. They, ironically, happened to also be having a party there, so she figured maybe she just didn't know some of the other guests. As time went on, it became more and more obvious she was in the wrong place. When she finally asked if the hostess was there, the neighbors laughed and said that she must be looking for the house next door. Embarrassed, she found the correct house, and upon seeing familiar faces greet her at the door, she knew she was in the right place.

Sometimes the blank on our invitation is "where?". For example, you know you're called to go on the mission field (the what), next year (the when), but you don't know where. The where is just as important as the when and the what. Take this example. Maybe you know God is calling you to higher education. Your applications to every university within a sixty-mile radius are turned down, and you're told to try to apply again next year. You return to God in prayer, and you receive confirmation that this is, in fact, the right timing. What you may have forgotten is to confirm the "where." Meanwhile, God had been preparing a both a move *and* the education experience you've been passionate about pursuing. Upon prayer and confirmation, you apply out of state and *bam!* You're accepted.

A good indicator of having the wrong "where" is that subtle feeling that you're in the wrong place. Just like my embarrassed friend, she began noticing little things like not knowing the other guests and not seeing our hostess. You may notice little signs that tell your spirit, "this is not the right place." If that's the case, don't forage ahead stubbornly ignoring them. Reassess. Conversely, when you are in the right place, you'll receive those reinforcements. Just like my friend seeing us when she rang the second doorbell, when you are in the right place, the things you see and hear will match with what God has told you.

GESTATION: THE WAIT

Sometimes, the answer isn't a move. We have the right location. The spiritual blank we are drawing is the blank of "when." When is God's timing? A heart can grow sick by filling in this blank prematurely. If we take a guess at when, and it's not God's timing, we watch our breakthrough time come and go. Too often we altogether throw out the promise because we have misinterpreted the timing.

Divine appointments are like babies. From the time they are conceived, it takes a preordained gestation process for them to grow, develop, and stretch us before they manifest to where we can see them. The problem this presents to our minds is that the incubation time for promises is wildly different. Sometimes it's decades. Other times it's days. Very occasionally, God will actually give you an appointed time to expect the manifestation. *Most times*, however, this is left blank. When we know what God has told us to expect and we have positioned ourselves in the place to receive it, our next job is to wait. You may wonder, "when is God's timing?" and the answer is sometimes no clearer than "not now."

I had been waiting for the timing of our second baby. Month after month came and went, and still nothing happened. Sitting on the floor next to a pile of tissues as I blubbered wondering if I could have more children, God then shared a word with me through the mouth of my husband. He told me that in the natural, special forces selection processes often require incredible physical tests that are just as much mental tests. For example, candidates may be asked to perform physical endurance tests for which they are not given the ending time. Think of being told to run without being told how far or for how long. As humans, we love to pace. When faced with an endless timeframe or endless distance, we quickly slip into giving up. Something happens, however, when the mental change is made to say, "I'm just going to run one step after another." No distance can phase you. No time length can beset you. *This* is what Paul meant when he told us as believers to run our race. It may be three steps or three hundred miles, but *when your decision to run is not contingent on it being less than a certain distance or time, you become spiritual special forces.* Instead of counting down, you begin building up. Each day—each step—becomes a building up towards the goal. Progress is felt in achieving the next step towards the timing instead of only being felt when the whole goal is achieved. We can't count down if we don't know the end date, but we can count how long we've been building. We also know the bigger the end result will be, the longer the build will take. If it hasn't happened yet, keep waiting. Don't give up. God just may be building something that was bigger than you previously estimated.

VOCATION: YOUR COMPASS

Sometimes the blank on our divine invitation is the event itself. This is that permanent state of anticipation where you can almost tangibly feel that "something" is about to happen, but you don't know what. Vocation literally originates from Latin, Old French, and Middle English roots meaning "to call." Maybe you know God is calling you to a place. Maybe you know God is saying the time is now. The question remains, though, of asking "What is supposed to happen?" or "What am I supposed to do, God?" These are actually two very different questions.

If you have been feeling God calling you, your first response is to ask God "what is my half?" With every divine appointment, there is something that is supposed to happen. This something may (or may not!) be something that requires partnering actions on your end. There is this divine blend in the miraculous of us doing what is *within* our power to do and God doing what is *beyond* our power to do. Many times, God is a God of meeting in the middle. Seeking your half sounds something like, "Lord, I pray that you reveal to me what you have placed within my power to do." While He *can*, and sometimes does, do everything Himself, we read in the testimonies in His word that He asks something of whomever He is choosing. He asked Jonah to go to Nineveh. He asked Joshua to march around Jericho. He asked Naaman wash in the Jordan. It would be a rather one-sided relationship if all that God ever planned for us happened *to* us. He plans, instead, to make things happen *with* us.

A friend gave me a birthday gift one year that she felt God was highlighting to her as a word for me. It was a canvas tote that read, "Live your life by a compass, not a clock" (a quote attributed to Stephen R. Covey). There is so much depth to this. A clock is mechanical and precise, ticking away at a steady and measurable rate. A compass is magnetic. It is *drawn* to a direction. It has nothing to do with a steady pace or measurable rate of progress. God has equipped us with our own spiritual compass. This compass is the Holy Spirit. When He sent His Spirit to us, it was with this commissioning:

> *"And I will ask the Father, and he will give you another advocate to help you and be with you forever—"*
>
> *John 14:16*

Just as a compass realigns with true north, the Holy Spirit reminds us of what He has spoken over us. It awakens the seeds in our hearts that were planted in our conception. Sometimes this could be in the form of a dream. Sometimes this could be in a persistent urge or unction. Other times this could be through God using someone as a mouthpiece to speak prophetic guidance to us. It could even be a passage of scripture that comes to life and breathes direction into our next moves. It's hard to precisely define, just as the pull of a compass is more abstract than the ticking of a clock. All we know is when we feel that draw towards doing something, we may have our "what."

DREAD

Dread is the enemy's knock-off of the anticipation and hopeful expectation we were meant to live with. We weren't meant to be blindly optimistic, but we were meant to know that troubles are the way are light and momentary when compared with the destinations. When we notice ourselves thinking "something is about to happen" and automatically we think that something may be bad, this is a sign of dread. When we notice ourselves filling in "never" or "a really long time" in the blank of timing rather pessimistically, this is a sign of dread. When we fear moving and all its troubles and downsides *more than* we look forward to what awaits us in the new places God has for us, this is a sign of dread. Dread is one letter off dead. There's a reason for that. This thinking kills your spirit. As you anticipate, don't let that anticipation lead to worry. Take each thought captive, and as you notice a dread response, flipped it back to the renewed-mind response.

As God renews our minds, we begin to look for invitations as things of great hope and fulfillment. We become aware that God is inviting us into divine appointments all the time. Once we begin to sense them, we look for what blanks are still unanswered. We seek. We use our Holy Spirit compass. We get into position. Make a habit of engaging God with questions. Ask Him, where are you calling me to serve right now? What is your timing? What are you calling me to do right now? Then begin to fill in your invitation blanks. Like a spiritual scavenger hunt, the completion of the invitation ends in a divine appointment that was well worth the seeking, doing, and waiting. When you view the unanswered through this renewed mind lens, even the waiting can be fun. Life then becomes a series of divine appointments.

As you continue your journey (because, as you may have noticed, this novel is rightly named an *ongoing* journey to a renewed mind), you are on the verge of your next divine appointment. How do I know? Our lives are a series of them. If you're not in one now, you're about to be. As you come to each new invitation, engage with the Lord. As you wait on His answers to sprout, like the first exciting bits of green poking over the dirt in your garden, wait with *hope*. Then the seeking can become just as delightful as the finding.

> Be patient, then, brothers and sisters, until the Lord's coming. See how the farmer waits for the land to yield its valuable crop, patiently waiting for the autumn and spring

rains. You too, be patient and stand firm, because the Lord's coming is near.

James 5:7–8

TAKE IT TO GOD:

Ask each of these questions one at a time, and wait in the still silence for God's answer. Jot it down!

What invitations are you giving me right now, God?
What are your words about my location right now?
What are your callings for me right now?
What words do you have for me regarding timing?

Epilogue

I COULD NEVER HAVE EXPECTED when I began this book the journey that it would be. It was almost like putting together a huge puzzle. God certainly also had me live every one of these chapters the hard way. Like anything God-inspired, this tool can be utilized by God different ways in different seasons. The questions you journal at the end of each chapter could and should change every season. This is also not an exhaustive list of all the aspects of renewing your mind, but my prayer is that it is a launching place for God to take those topics deeper and branch out in ways a book could never contain. I pray these words will help you triumph over double-mindedness, ways of the world, hopelessness, and every other mental hurdle to running your race. I pray sharing with you these experiences will spark your own journey of discovering the backwards thinking of heaven. Like ripples going out from a single drop, then what God does *through you* will ripple out to the ends of the earth.

Blessings,

Bibliography

Cambridge Dictionary. 2021. https://dictionary.cambridge.org/.

Merriam-Webster.com. 2011. https://www.merriam-webster.com.

Strong, James. *Strong's Expanded Exhaustive Concordance of the Bible*. Nashville: Thomas Nelson, 2009. Print.

www.ingramcontent.com/pod-product-compliance
Lightning Source LLC
Chambersburg PA
CBHW060351090426
42734CB00011B/2106